ENDURING

FRIENDSHIPS

D1717033

Bill Thon

ENDURING FRIENDSHIPS

Edited by
AL ROBERTS

Written by ROGER F. DUNCAN, HERALD
JONES, JOHN GOULD, MALCOLM BARTER,
AL ROBERTS, EDWARD W. COFFIN, CY
HAMLIN, AND JAMES S. ROCKEFELLER, JR.

CARLTON SIMMONS, Official Photographer

with Notes from
BILL THON'S
Sketchbook

with a Foreword by
HOWARD I. CHAPELLE

Published for the FRIENDSHIP SLOOP SOCIETY
by the INTERNATIONAL MARINE PUBLISHING CO.
Camden, Maine

DATE DUE			
GAYLORD			PRINTED IN U.S.A.

To the people and friends of Friendship who recognized the excellence of the Friendship Sloop and labored that a hundred Friendships might today be sailing.

CONTENTS

FOREWORD

The rejuvenation of a type of small Maine Coast fishing sloop, considered obsolete by yachtsmen as far back as 1915, may now be taken as recognition of the good qualities of the type, the Friendship Sloop. This was accomplished by the Friendship Sloop Society, formed at Friendship, Maine, in 1961. Originally intended only as a means of bringing together the surviving Friendship Sloops and their owners for a three-day regatta, it was not long before the Society found itself engaged in research on the history of the type and in a search for sources of half-models, plans and data on the builders of the sloops. As a result, the Society is now a repository for a wide range of information on the Friendship Sloop, as this book shows.

Another result of the Friendship Sloop Society's efforts has been to encourage the construction of new Friendship Sloops, ranging from faithful replicas of the old fishing sloops to yachts having some resemblance to a Friendship Sloop.

The efforts of the Society also led to the repair and preservation of old sloops; often this amounted to almost complete rebuilding of an old boat. By these means, a growing number of Friendship Sloops are appearing, and interest is increasing; perhaps we may shortly see sloops built by mass-production methods, using either fiberglass or ferro-concrete construction.

This book will give a reader a complete account of the history and development of the Friendship Sloop, and of their builders—and appreciation for what the Friendship Sloop Society has accomplished.

HOWARD I. CHAPELLE

PREFACE

It was inevitable in view of the modern-day interest in boating that Friendship Sloops should return to the limelight in boating circles. A more seaworthy and dependable boat is difficult to find. They make wonderful boats for family sailing and endear themselves to the hearts of the traditionally minded.

It was in 1961 that the Friendship Sloop Society was founded, primarily through the efforts of Bernard MacKenzie, a proud Sloop owner from Scituate, Massachusetts. Flushed with the excitement of winning a Boston Power Squadron Race with his old, original, Morse-built, Friendship Sloop, *Voyager*, Bernard dreamed a dream of a race for Friendship Sloops only. Through a procession of contacts including Earl Banner, John Gould, Carlton Simmons, and Herald Jones, the Friendship Sloop Society was born in April of 1961 with nearly two dozen enthusiasts in Friendship on deck to lend a hand with preparations for the first race. Headed by Herald Jones, this small group did the nearly impossible, and held the first Friendship Sloop Regatta on July 22nd, 1961.

From this modest but highly successful beginning, the Society has grown and prospered. A regatta for Friendship Sloops has been held on the last weekend in July each year. While 14 boats raced in 1961, the fleet bearing down on the starting line in 1969 numbered 34. At this writing, the Society has over 200 members, and nearly 100 registered Friendship Sloops. Incidentally, you don't have to own a Friendship Sloop to be a member of the Society; many people from the far corners of the world interested in the preservation and sailing of the type, in traditional boats in general, or people who just plain appreciate a good boat have been welcomed to membership.

At the Skipper's Meeting of the 1967 Regatta, Bill Pendleton proposed that the Friendship Sloop Society create a scholarship fund, part of which would go into endowment and part into direct grants to Friendship boys and girls who need financial help for post-high-school education.

The proposition was carried out with such success that in 1968 three grants were made, two to students at Gorham State Teachers College and one to a student at Thomas College. In 1969, we increased the endowment fund and were able to help one student to go to Aurora College, one to Thomas College, and one to the Maine School of Nursing.

In 1968, the fund was named the Beatrice Pendleton Scholarship Fund in memory of Mrs. William Pendleton, whose efforts and enthusi-

"A regatta for Friendship Sloops has been held on the last weekend in July each year."

asm had done much to get the fund started and who died suddenly that spring.

Vigorous efforts are made annually to call the membership's attention to the Fund. Many skippers make a practice of giving to the Fund 10 per cent of their fitting-out expenses. Seilers has provided the Annual Skippers Banquet on the evening of Friendship Day without cost, thus permitting the total receipts from tickets to go into the Fund.

Through its intertest in Friendship Sloops, the Society seeks to appreciate and preserve the spirit that inspired the craftsmanship, pride, and independence characteristic of Maine and particularly of Friendship. In the modern world, this spirit cannot be effectively expressed without education. The Society feels it is important to help youngsters gain the means of contributing their talents to a world badly in need of them.

Along with the birth and growth of the Friendship Sloop Society, an independent but kindred activity has taken place that is worthy of mention here. Just one year prior to the birth of the Society, an idea for a Friendship Museum began to take shape in the mind of Al Roberts, a local lobster dealer. Al had accumulated a few interesting odds and ends pertinent to the his-

tory of Friendship. He had half models, some old tools and implements, and a unique collection of lobster measures, including one of every size that had ever been used since the first Maine lobster conservation law was passed in 1872.

Al was just about to open up a room on his wharf to display this memorabilia of the town, when he decided that such a project should be an undertaking for the whole town rather than for an individual, so the idea was temporarily shelved. With the beginning of the Friendship Sloop Society, there was new interest in the town and a new pride in its heritage. With this impetus, the Friendship Museum, Incorporated, was formed and in June, 1964, the Museum opened its doors to the public for the first time.

The Museum is housed in a building that should itself be in a museum. It is a one-room brick schoolhouse that was used for eight grades from 1851 to 1923. Many of the townspeople remember having learned their three R's there. The building was sold to the Condon family after it was abandoned as a school, and since that time has occasionally been used as a community gathering place during the summer months. The Foster family, who inherited the structure, loaned it to Friendship Museum, Incorporated, for a three-year period. Since that

4

Red Boutilier

time the Museum has grown and prospered, and the three-year lease has been extended, on a dollar-a-year basis.

The townspeople responded to requests for loans and gifts, and the Museum now contains all sorts of artifacts pertaining to the history of Friendship. At the end of the second year, the old schoolhouse was ready to burst at the seams. Because of the history of the building itself, nothing has been done about moving to larger quarters. Much of the charm of the Museum is due to the little old schoolhouse.

While old Sloop models and half models of Friendship-built lobster boats occupy a prominant part of the display, this Museum is not only a marine museum. It encompasses all phases of life in Friendship, but naturally the sea has played a predominant part in the life of every Friendshipper all the way back to the Indians.

The Friendship Sloop Society has printed a program for each of its regattas. The first was an eight-page booklet, and the most recent one contains 80 pages. These programs have presented and preserved considerable information on the Sloops and many photographs of them. Early in the Society's existence, the printing of these programs was seen to be a valuable part of the Society's objective of encouraging sailing

Friendship Sloops and letting people know about these excellent boats.

In 1962, therefore, a more ambitious publishing project was undertaken. *Ships That Came Home*, a 44-page, soft-bound book was prepared by members of the Society and printed in an edition of 500 copies. These books are now collectors' items. A larger hard-cover book was brought out by the Society in 1965, *It's A Friendship*, a volume of 95 pages that made available further data and new photographs of Friendship Sloops. Two printings of 2,000 copies sold out readily.

Consequently, in 1969, we began work on this, our third book. Like its predecessors, this book has no single author. It is the result of the efforts of many people joined to make what we hope is a fairly complete story of Friendship Sloops. We have called upon the knowledge, ability, and cooperative spirit of many people to bring this book about. All the leading photographers in the Friendship area have been most generous in offering us their pictures to supplement those taken by Carlton Simmons, the official photographer of the Friendship Sloop Society. Owners, builders, and designers have let us pick their brains, and writers have given of their talents.

With nautical experts like Howard Chapelle, Jay Hanna, Geerd Hendel, and Winnie Lash helping us, and known writers like John Gould, Roger Duncan, Jim Rockefeller, and Malcolm Barter adding their efforts, not to mention major contributions by Herald Jones, Ed Coffin, Bill Thon, and Betty Roberts, and important contributions by many too numerous to mention, it is with a feeling that we have had the help of the very best available talent that we bring this book to you.

THE FRIENDSHIP SLOOP SOCIETY
GEORGE BURNHAM MORRILL, JR., President
WILLIAM PENDLETON, Vice President
BETTY ROBERTS, Secretary
CARLTON SIMMONS, Treasurer
WILLIAM S. DANFORTH, Chairman,
    Race Committee
AL ROBERTS, Chairman, Program Committee

I

WHAT IS A FRIENDSHIP?

by ROGER F. DUNCAN

Wilbur Morse defined a Friendship Sloop as "a sloop built in Friendship, Maine, by Wilbur Morse." He should know. He probably built more of them than anyone else.

Winfield Lash, of Lash Brothers' Yard at the head of Hatchet Cove in Friendship, defines a Friendship Sloop as one that follows exactly a half model he has. It was made by Wilbur Morse and given to Winnie by Miss Eda Lawry, granddaughter of Mr. Morse. It is said to be the ultimate refinement of the Friendship model. Winnie says that a Friendship Sloop must have the hollow bow and the hollow garboards of the model. The drag and rocker of the keel must be the same. She must have an overhanging counter with a transom which does not drag in the water, and the buttock lines must not be flat, but curved slightly upward to meet the counter. The prismatic coefficient and water-line coefficient must not vary from the model. In short, says Winnie, whether larger or smaller than the 37-foot sloop originally built from it, a Friendship Sloop must preserve the true proportions of this model.

Lash Brothers built the *Mary Anne, Downeaster, Dirigo,* and *Rights of Man* from this model, but raised the sides a little to provide headroom below. They were very close to the Morse model.

However, Maine in general and the Friendship region in particular abound with old-timers who speak of Friendship Sloops built by Charles Morse, Abdon Carter, the McLains, and Albion Morse, as well as by many others. They contest hotly the claim that Wilbur Morse built the only Friendship Sloop or the first one or the best one.

The design originated from the Muscongus Bay sloop, a clipper-bowed, lapstrake or carvel planked boat with a centerboard, seldom over twenty-eight feet long, used to haul lobster traps among the ledges. Many were built at Bremen and on Bremen Long Island, as well as at many other coves and harbors up and down the Bay. The success of the Edward Burgess designed Gloucester fisherman *Fredonia* with her cutaway underbody and easy sections produced a smaller adaptation, the Gloucester sloop boat. The combination of this with the Muscongus Bay sloop produced the traditional Friendship Sloop.

She was admirably adapted to her trade. High and sharp forward, she seldom was stopped by a sea and she kept her crew relatively dry. Her broad waist made a comfortable and stable working platform, and her low sides and narrow deck made lifting fish and lobster traps aboard relatively easy. The cockpit floor was

7

" . . . you will notice that her bow is very fine; indeed it is actually concave in section. This hollow in the bow runs aft under the boat and increases as it goes. As you approach the stern you will find that in cross section the boat turns in sharply just below the waterline, runs almost flat, with little deadrise until nearly the middle of the boat, and then turns down to quite a deep keel, often with a lead or iron shoe." (The *Windward* and *Sazerac*.)

often laid loosely so water could drain into the bilge and thence be pumped out. She was usually ballasted with rocks. Her mast was far forward so that she would handle easily under mainsail alone, and, to fan home in Maine's gentle summer breezes, she often carried topsails and jibs set on a long bowsprit. However, shortened down with reefed mainsail, she was stiff enough to get her crew home in a winter blow.

Now these old Sloops are all gone, or are substantially changed by rebuilding. It has been said that he who owns an original Friendship owns "a pair of trail boards, a pile of rot, and a damned good pump." Perhaps the best way to understand a modern Friendship Sloop and her heritage is to come to Friendship on the last weekend in July and see some for yourself at the Friendship Sloop Society's annual Friendship Sloop Regatta.

You will find a fleet of upwards of 30 Sloops which will all look similar, yet each will have her unique qualities. All are gaff-rigged. Almost all have two jibs, the outer one set on a bow-

"The Skipper, intent less on speed than on avoiding a gybe which might dismast his crew, still has time to admire the smooth wake astern." (The *Downeaster.*)

sprit. All have the graceful clipper bow from which the line of the rail swings aft to a low point at the cockpit and turns up gracefully to a rounded stern. If you find one grounded out on the tide across from Al Roberts' wharf, you will notice that her bow is very fine; indeed it is actually concave in section. This hollow in the bow runs aft under the boat and increases as it goes. As you approach the stern, you will find that in cross section the side of the boat turns in sharply just below the water line, runs almost flat, with little deadrise, until nearly the middle of the boat, and then turns down to quite a deep keel, often with a lead or iron shoe.

With these general characteristics the similarities between boats cease. Friendship Sloops

9

Martin Leifer

" . . . he may be planning a trip aloft in a boatswain's chair to put a shackle behind the upper peak halyard block to take the twist out of it." (Bill Thon aboard the *Echo*.)

range in size from less than 20 to more than 40 feet. Some, like the old timers, have the mast far forward with tremendous mainsails and small headsails. Others have been built with the mast farther aft and with the mainsail reduced to make them easier to handle. Some have topmasts, gaff topsails and jib topsails—still invaluable in light summer weather. Some have large cockpits and small cabins, and some, in the interest of comfortable cruising, have long, high cabin houses. One even has a little penthouse on top of the cabin to give the owner full headroom over his stove. Some steer with a tiller and some with a wheel. Shining paint, clear varnish, teak decks and hand-rubbed interiors contrast sharply with flat paint and locker doors with whittled wooden buttons. One may have spreader lights illuminating the decks at night, and another will be but a shadow dimly defined by a smoky lantern in the starboard rigging.

Perhaps we shall find characteristics in the owner which will shed some light on the character of the boat. Behold him sitting on the wheel-box running up Friendship harbor before the gentle afternoon southwester. He will be clad in work pants, whatever shirt was at hand, a jacket perhaps saved from the skiing season, and a cap designed to keep the sun out of a fisherman's eyes. The main sheet is trimmed about right, but we see no one slacking off an inch or two at the sharp command of an eagle-eyed skipper. The crew, usually family, is likely to be sitting around the cockpit or on top of the house, talking, taking pictures, waving to

"When the guns begin to bang from the *White Falcon's* stern, the windward end of the starting line seems to be the one place on the coast of Maine that the skipper wants to be. An iron determination and a haziness about the barging rules can produce a real jam at this spot."

friends, or tanning themselves in the sun. The skipper, intent less on speed than on avoiding a gybe which might dismast his crew, still has time to admire the smooth wake astern. Perhaps subconsciously, he is aware, too, of a scar on the starboard side of the deck where his son made a major miscalculation in learning to heave a sounding lead, and he may be planning a trip aloft in a bosun's chair to put a shackle behind the upper peak halyard block to take the twist out of it.

The Society's official cannoneer on the wharf welcomes the newcomer with a salvo and the fleet responds with horns and shouts. Our skipper warns of a gybe, gathers in the main sheet hand over hand, swings the mainsail across, suggests that his second son douse the jib, rounds into the wind and watches his first son ease the anchor over the bow as the little vessel hangs in the wind, her reef points tapping.

The mainsail comes down as neatly as a gull folds its wings, and there she is.

A red flag with a white T on it, signifying that visitors are welcome to tea, is tied to a starboard shroud and friends come aboard, usually in families. They are more likely to travel in cut-down dories, lapstreak skiffs, punts, or peapods than in the plastic eggshells usually used as yacht tenders, and oars are more common than outboards.

What do these people talk about? Not of ocean passages, of great gales in southern latitudes, of trade winds or artic ice. The talk runs on how hard it is to hear Mark Island fog signal to the westward; the ranges on a good spot for codfish off Monhegan ("Run east from the bell until you drop the lighthouse in the trees"), a little-known anchorage off Jonesport; or a harrowing experience making Portland Light-ship in the fog along with a tanker. Perhaps the

11

"The skipper of a Friendship Sloop loves the sweep of her sheer, the way she sits on the water, the slightly dumpy, business-like look of her." (The *Downeaster*.)

talk will turn to those who have built their own boats—of the problems of lofting, of finding good oak for knees or pine for decks, of the relative virtues of dead-eyes and turnbuckles to set up rigging. Some one may open up the question of fiberglass versus wood construction and start an argument that will last all evening and will lead into a discussion of the next day's race.

In the morning, observe a change in our normally easy-going skipper and his relaxed crew. As soon as the racing number is lashed in the shrouds, we see a profound interest in setting up rigging and pulling sails out tightly on spars. We see one boy rowing ashore to find something that will do for a whisker pole and another diving overboard to be sure the pro-peller is lined up with the rudder to reduce drag.

When the guns begin to bang from the *White Falcon's* stern, the windward end of that starting line seems to be the one place on the coast of Maine that the skipper wants to be. An iron determination and a haziness about the barging rules can produce a real jam at this spot. After the start, as the fleet spreads out a bit, perhaps a sharp luffing match will develop. As four Sloops converge on the windward mark, each moving fast and weighing upwards of five tons, it is a miracle that nothing more than paint is damaged. Does the course go pretty close to the end of Hall's Island? "Hold on till you see bottom," is the inflexible command. Bus Mosbacher is no more canny a skipper.

Elmer Barde

"A Friendship Sloop is a state of mind composed of independence, tradition, resourcefulness . . . " (The *Downeaster*.)

Yet after the race, the competitive fire dies, and the conversation in the cockpits turns to raising money for the Society's Scholarship Fund, or perhaps to national politics. If it is a heated discussion, it is likely to be about pollution of New England waters.

The skipper of a Friendship Sloop loves the sweep of her sheer, the way she sits on the water, the slightly dumpy, business-like look of her. She was designed to earn her living lobstering and fishing year round in these waters and

she looks it. If he has not actually built her himself, her owner has probably painted and rigged her. The splices and whippings are his. The lead of the staysail sheet is his invention. He may have fashioned the cleats and mast hoops, because it is almost impossible to buy them nowadays.

You don't acquire a Friendship Sloop by looking at a brochure, asking a salesman, "How much does that one cost?" and saying, "I'll take one of those." If you can find one for sale, you

13

will have to go over her with a sharp eye and an icepick. Is there rot in the stern, in the transom, in the partners, in the mast step? Is she hogged with age? Who built her? Who rebuilt her? Who made her sails? Can she accommodate a family of four? How good is her pump? Does the engine run when called upon? Does the peapod go with her? Is there a compass deviation card? Is she dry going to windward in a chop? And most important of all, how much does she leak? After a suitable financial arrangement is made, the new owner doesn't really own the boat until he has sailed her a season, sewed a new clew in the jib, found a throat halyard block in the basement junk heap of an Atlantic Avenue ship chandlery, and broken the spirit of the recalcitrant engine. The boat becomes part of him and he becomes part of the boat because he likes it that way.

She is not so fast to windward as some of the tall racing sloops, nor so stiff in a breeze. But start sheets, and on a reach she will surprise some of the modern gold platers. Running off the wind in a sea, she will steer easily and be dry and steady. She will want a reef in the mainsail when it comes on to blow, but she will get her owner and his family home relatively dry, comfortable, and unafraid. If he bumps her on a ledge—everyone does—it probably won't hurt her much and the tide will lift her off. If something breaks, he can mend it himself. He can take a large party aboard comfortably or he can sail her alone. Peace is undisturbed by the howl of sheet on winch or the nervous vagaries of a masthead spinnaker. She will lie to an anchor like a tired duck and will heave to at sea in comfort.

A Friendship Sloop is a gaff-rigged sloop with a fisherman look about her. A Friendship Sloop is a beautiful fusion of form and function. A Friendship Sloop is a state of mind composed of independence, tradition, resourcefulness, and a most fortuitous combination of geography and language in the name Friendship.

II

TALKING FRIENDSHIPS

by Herald A. Jones

I was dog-tired that night as I left the skippers' meeting, but everything was ready for the start of the Friendship Sloop Regatta the next day. As I drove home past the harbor, I slowed and gazed at all those Sloops there in the moonlight with a sense of real satisfaction, for I had helped to bring them together—back to Friendship where they were born.

Just boats, of course, even fat and squatty looking, as they rode at anchor, but I knew that tomorrow, as they raised their white wings to the breeze, a sudden metamorphosis would take place, and each would become a thing of real beauty. Jim Rockefeller was right: they did have "character." As work boats, they had helped to develop the economy of the Maine Coast; they were part of the land and it's people.

The closing words of the speaker of the evening came to me; "If these boats could talk, they'd have many a tale to tell of their part in the growth of the fishing industry along the New England coast." As I dozed off to sleep that night, those words of the speaker came again: "If these boats could talk . . . "

I don't know how long it was before I found the moon shining in my face, and those same words throbbing in my head, "If these boats could talk, if these boats could talk, If these . . . "

I knew my sleep was over for the time being, so I pulled on some clothes, lifted the canoe from it's rack and slipped it into the quiet water. Paddling had calmed my nerves before, so why not? The moon was full, the world asleep, and just around the point lay more Friendship Sloops than had ever been seen together, even in the old days.

Lazy strokes soon brought them into view. How quiet they were in the bright moonlight. Soundlessly I drifted among them, recognizing Sloops which had returned for the Regatta so frequently: the *Black Jack, Dirigo, Chrissy, Eastward, Depression, Chance, Vida Mia, Ellie T, Content, Rights of Man*, and so many others. Some old favorites were missing, of course: the *Voyager*, whose owner Bernard McKenzie had dreamed up the Regatta; *Jolly Buccaneer*, now owned in Florida; *Wanderer*, whose owners had caused so much gaiety in years past, and many others. Yet there were new boats to take their places—more than ever before. Old friend and stranger alike, they were personages, each an entity to be reckoned with. From tip of mast to water line; from clipper bow to eliptical stern, these old work-horses were clothed in dignity—an integrity that a pure pleasure boat could never have.

I noted the loving touches their skippers had

15

Courtesy, James S. Rockefeller

"Just boats, of course, even fat and squatty looking, as they rode at anchor, but I knew that tomorrow, as they raised their white wings to the breeze, a sudden metamorphosis would take place, and each would become a thing of real beauty." (The *Windward, Ellie T, Eastward,* and *Heritage.*)

given them so they might appear to good advantage in the Regatta tomorrow. Well, their skippers were taking their well-earned rest now, judging by the sounds from within the cabins. Occasionally I thought I made out a word, and I smiled as I thought, "Someone talks in his sleep." I quit paddling, sat motionless, and then became conscious of a sort of mumbled conversation going on from boat to boat; as

I listened, more words became audible, but still I could see no one talking.

It made no sense at all; if the Sloops weren't talking, who was? And suddenly I knew. They could talk; they were talking now!

"Ahoy." I waited for an answer. None came. Then again, "Ahoy! Ahoy the canoe!"

"Wh- wh- gulp." I was speechless.

"Hey! You in the canoe!"

"You mean *me?*"

"Yes, you. Didn't you help establish our Regatta?"

"Ye-e-s,' sort of." I was still breathless.

"And aren't you writing something for the new book the Society is publishing?"

"Yes." One word was all I could manage.

"Then listen carefully. We are proud that we were work boats, and we want to tell you about it, so you'll get it straight. You'll find a pad and pencil on the taff-rail of the *Depression* just ahead of you, so you can take notes."

I found the pad, resumed my seat and proclaimed myself ready. Then, one after another of the Sloops told of the work each had done. The *Depression*, being the oldest present—1899 —began the tale.

In the early days the fishermen couldn't range so far as they can now, didn't have the boats to do it. Peapods, and later, dories, had to be rowed and weren't big enough to carry many traps. They rigged them with sails of sorts, but the boats were too small, and the best fishing grounds were usually very crowded.

Hand-lining for cod and pollock paid pretty well then, and Monhegan was frequently mentioned as a favorite location for hand-lining— lots of cod, pollock, haddock, and hake there. Wilbur Morse wrote in his journals that whenever somebody started to haul in fish, all the others would crowd around until one could almost walk from one boat to another. So he designed and built a nineteen-footer and put sail on her so he could range farther and find new territories to fish.

"Some remembered the *Annie Margie*, a 41-footer built by Wilbur Morse that took parties out."

He always claimed he caught more fish than anybody, but his sloop-boats were so popular with the fishermen that he could do better building than fishing, so he quit fishing. And he wasn't the only one: the Carters, the McLains, the other Morses, and many others would build a sloop-boat during the winter months and use her for hand-lining and setting trawls during the summer, then sell her and build another the following winter.

Fishing has changed a lot since then. In order to get away from crowded fishing areas, people lived on the islands and would fish as far as their boats could reach from there. The islands were apt to get the wind earlier than the harbor, too, so they could start work earlier. That was quite an advantage.

A man could only haul about 60 traps a day if he lobstered. Back in those days, they couldn't buy red-fish for bait like they do now, so fishermen had to catch their own bait after hauling traps all day. They used cunners, herring-filled

17

N. L. Stebbins, courtesy, the Society for the Preservation of New England Antiques

"The Sloops who had done it claimed that swordfishing was real sport. One of the men would take the harpoon out on the bowsprit and balance there until he got his fish. He could never have done it with an unsteady boat under him." (*Olive E.*)

bait bags, flounders, tails from short lobsters. They would set nets for cunners in places where the bottom showed light in color. John Lash, "Old Bob's" father, was the first to rig a drag to catch flounders for bait.

Here let me quote an exchange between the *Sazarac* and *Black Jack* verbatim: "I miss that

old sweet smell of bait since we quit fishing. They'd catch a lot of flounders or cunners and let them ripen for two or three days. Man, didn't they smell good!"

"You didn't look so spic-an-span clean then as you do now, though."

"That's true. The men didn't have much time left to keep us painted up. But I'd shed a coat of paint any day if I could get rid of these stinkin' gasoline engines they're using in us now. Of all the foul-smelling, noisy messes they bring aboard! Give me that good, clean bait smell any day."

The Sloops that were used for party boats

18

had to be scrubbed down before the passengers came aboard; *they* didn't like the bait smell. Sloops make good party boats because the wide beam and hard bilges keep them from heeling too much, the high, flaring bow keeps the passengers dry, and the weight and easy lines give a gentle motion that's good for landlubber stomachs. They're fast enough to be fun, too.

Some remembered the *Annie Margie,* a 41-footer built by Wilbur Morse that took parties out. For that matter, it was common practice to scrub Sloops down and take a party of summer folks off on a picnic.

One of the early *Sunshine* boats of the Maine Sea Coast Missionary Society was a sloop-boat back in 1905. They visited the off-shore islands and hauled lots of people—sick folks and islanders that had to come to the mainland for some reason.

One of the recently-built boats asked a pertinent question: "How could one man handle a Sloop and get his traps hauled at the same time?"

"If you'd stop to think, you wouldn't have to ask," said the *Chrissy.* "When you come up to your buoy, your skipper leads out the main sheet quite a ways, and trims the jib tight. You'd lay there good, wouldn't you?"

"Well, yes, I guess I would."

"And with the wind astern, your man would gybe you round and lead out the main sheet, and you'd lay there meek as a kitten, while he hauled his trap."

"Sure, that's just what would come natural to us. But sposin' my man fetched up too close to a ledge?"

"That happened plenty of times. That's why our builders put such heavy timbers in us. Most times, it didn't hurt us a bit. Of course, with our deep draft, they couldn't get as close in as they can with their present boats, but it was surprising how close they did get. In winter, the men liked to pair up and take a dory along. One would stay in the Sloop while the other hauled the traps. On real cold days, one man would stay in the cuddy until he'd see his partner's nose start to turn white. Then it was time to change places."

Someone recalled the custom of "jogging," wherein the men took a young lad along and towed a dory out to the good fishing grounds. The men would climb into the dory and fish with hand-lines and the boy would jog back and forth in the Sloop, keeping the dory in sight while the men fished. The boys loved it, and it saved the men heaving the long anchor line in at the end of the day. Of course, once in a while the fog would come in and give the lad a real fright, but there was never a real-for-sure tragedy.

More than one Sloop spoke of how they used to seine for mackerel. The men liked the large Sloops for that. They remembered how Allie Cushman's father used his 48-foot *North Star* for seining. It was an interesting operation, too. When they reached a school of mackerel, the Sloop would be hove to and allowed to drift while the men spread toll as far as they could throw it. Then the seine would be dropped overboard all around the boat. One man would be sent out on the bowsprit with a long pole with an oarlock tied to the end. The jib was run up, and the man on the bowsprit would hold the net down low while the Sloop sailed out of the net. Then the purse would be drawn, and the catch hauled aboard and taken ashore to sell. They recalled that the 38-foot *Wilbur Morse* (not the replica now sailing) was used for seining clear up off Block Island and New Bedford.

The Sloops who had done it claimed that swordfishing was real sport. One of the men would take the harpoon out on the bowsprit and balance there till he got his fish. He could never have done it with an unsteady boat under him. Charlie Dodge used to take the *Mary J. Beale* and the *North Star* swordfishing even as far down as Cape Breton Island. One time he brought in 30,000 pounds of swordfish, the largest one 700 pounds and the smallest, 100 pounds, and they sold for eight cents a pound!

Someone asked if Sloops had ever been used as lobster smacks, and was told that this required a Sloop especially constructed for the purpose. Two water-tight bulkheads were built in, creating a "well" amidships. Then one-and-a-half-inch holes were bored in the planking until there was nearly as much area in holes as in planking, allowing sea water to flow in and out as the Sloop moved. Lobsters were dumped through a four-foot hatch and thus were kept alive as the boat was under way. These boats had a little less freeboard, but otherwise handled the same as ordinary Sloops.

The *Depression* summed it all up: "With so many families living on the islands, we were called upon to carry a lot of freight in between our fishing chores—freight that could be stowed in the cuddy or low in the cockpit so it wouldn't interfere with the sails. All in all, I think you'll agree that we served our time in history well."

"Indeed, we all agree," said the *Dirigo*, "and I'm sure we'll cherish the fact that, though we came too late to serve the needs you originals filled, we are built off the same lines and are true Friendships. Who knows, now that the world is in such a frenetic mess, but that our sturdiness, steadiness, and quiet strength will aid our owners and their families and friends in keeping their reason and, in the long run, serve to build good will and peace."

I was thinking what a nice speech that was, and beginning to feel a sense of pride in our Sloop Society—after all, what the world needs is more Friendships!—when I realized the first spokesman was calling again: "Have you heard what we've been saying?"

"Every word. I've made complete notes."

"And you'll put it all in your book?"

"I promise—just as you have told it. I might add that this has been an unusual opportunity for me."

"Never mind the compliments, just get paddling. If you don't get home before the moon sets, you'll lose both your glass slippers, as well as your notes."

As I dipped my paddle and pointed the canoe toward the great red disk that was the moon, I thought I heard a friendly chuckling among the fleet. Suddenly, I chuckled too. I was a distinguished personage. Was I not the only man in history who ever carried on a conversation with a fleet of Friendship Sloops?

Morning came, and my returning senses recalled my unbelievable adventure of the moonlit hours. I dressed hurriedly and went out to the canoe rack. I passed my fingers over the canvas and they came away smudged with the dust of disuse. I went to the boat house and examined my paddle: dusty!

Only a dream. Well, I still had to write that chapter for the book. I closed the boat house door, went to my study, sharpened my pencils, rolled up my sleeves and sat down at my desk. There, in front of me was a pad of scribbled notes about Friendship Sloops!

III

NAMING FRIENDSHIPS

by John Gould

Friendship is a lovely word to use for a town name. How did it come about?

In the Bible, Adam had the task of naming all things, but his day was long done before he got around to the Indian names of the Province of Maine, so we can't blame Meduncook on him. There are two ways of explaining Indian names. One is the euphonic; in this instance the story goes that for a big feast the head chief of the Abnaki tribe set a bunch of boys to digging clams, whereat the first to fill his hod came up and said, "Me done, cook!" and thus the place was named. The second way is to convert derived orthography back into basic Indian and find out what the word meant in the beginning.

Meduncook thus seems to mean, in Indian, "Place by tide where sun shines over islands and warriors make beautiful canoes." As a name for that section of the Maine coast later to become Friendship, Meduncook served long after the Indians became unimportant, through the colonial days, and into the 19th century.

There isn't much record of the precise conversations that took place when the folks who had become established here decided to select another name and give up the old Meduncook, but one story goes that a vessel came into the harbor and tied up at a wharf and somebody was struck by the appropriateness of her name. Across her stern were the letters: *Friendship*.

"There," said the somebody, "that's a good name for a town!"

Meduncook became Friendship.

There is historical evidence that this *could* have happened. At least three vessels named *Friendship* were afloat at about that time, and any of them *might* have put into Meduncook. The least likely of the three would have been the first, for she was a little early, but historically she had a certain importance.

Built in Portland, this first *Friendship* (not a Friendship Sloop, of course, but a trading vessel named *Friendship*) wound up in the Sumatra pepper trade. She belongs in that period between the American Revolution and the War of 1812—the grand days of Maine maritime adventure and success. One day off Quallah Battoo (Gesundheit!) this pepper ship was attacked and captured by Malays. That was the end of her, but to avenge this piracy Captain John Downes of the frigate *Potomac* stormed Quallah Battoo and put it out of business. He killed the Sultan Po Mahomet and 150 of his men, destroyed the forts, and burned the place. Thus the *Friendship* touched off Uncle Sam's first naval engagement in the Pacific Ocean.

More likely to have figured in the naming

"Meduncook thus seems to mean, in Indian, 'Place by tide where sun shines over islands . . . ' "

of Friendship was the second vessel of that name—a Portland-built schooner that did considerable coasting. Those were the days of the "press gangs," and this *Friendship* figured in one sticky incident at Kingston, Jamaica. France and England were in a fuss, and England desperately needed men for her warships. Not about, pleasantly, to give up her contention that she was queen of the seas, England was raiding Yankee vessels pretty much at will, and in high-handed fashion. Almost every ship of the line had some poor soul from Maine aboard—there was even Sylvanus Snow of Orrington aboard Nelson's vessel at Trafalgar. So it wasn't at all unusual to have a boarding party show up and take some men. Maine skippers and seamen had papers, but the British didn't pay much attention to them. Their gimmick was to claim these Maine sailors were skedaddled British tars.

So when Captain Smith was in Kingston Harbor with his *Friendship,* the limeys came aboard and took everybody in his crew except his first mate. Until he could round up a few new hands Captain Smith dallied in Kingston. 'Tis said that the British officer who 'pressed Captain Smith's crew insisted that everybody strip, so he could see if they had flog marks on their backs. Any sign of a beating was sure proof the lad had been in the British Ny-vee! It was pretty hard in those days to find anybody on the coast of Maine who had a good word for the English, and probably Captain Smith added to the matter when he got home and told that story.

Another Maine skipper who was mixed up in this impressment of seamen several times was a Captain Theodore Wells of the town of Wells. One of his stories may show the average speed of British naval officers in that period. When the boarding party arrived the 'press-gang officer said, "Where do you hail from?"

Captain Wells said, "Wells."

"Aha!" said the officer. "What did I tell you —Welshmen!"

This Captain Wells later came to command the third of the *Friendships* which may have named the town. She was built in Wells, and one of her voyages was a symphony in frustration that may sound to certain Sloop owners like their own adventures in Handicap Alley. Captain Smith cleared from Wells with a cargo of hewn timbers, bound for St. Vincent. He was told by his owners not to dispose of his cargo unless he could get 100 gallons of molasses for each 1,000 board feet of lumber. That made sense, for those were the days of New England rum, and West Indian molasses was in high demand. The *Friendship* made a quick passage, but Captain Wells found he couldn't make any such favorable trade in St. Vincent, so he pushed on. A part of his journal is included in *A Maritime History of Maine* by William H. Rowe:

"From St. Vincent I sailed for Grenada where not finding a market from thence I left for Trinidad where I was still unable to effect a sale. Proceeding northward I touched at Port Royal in the island of Martinico. Here I failed to find a satisfactory sale. From this port I proceeded to Bastarre in the Island of Guadaloupe where the same disappointment waited me. I next touched at Nevis but could not dispose of my freight without trusting it in hands of doubtful solvency. From here I sailed for St. Thomas. At this point there was no demand for a cargo like mine. I attempted to reach Puerto Rico which was the last island where molasses was to be found excepting Cuba but in this failed because of a fresh blow and thick stormy weather which drove me by it when I ran for Aquin in the Island of St. Domingo and here as elsewhere I found a dull market and no sale."

The odyssey was just starting. He sailed on and on with his timbers, looking for molasses. He ran from San Domingo to Aux Cayes, to Jérémie, to Mariguana, and to Port-au-Prince. Everywhere he found he had been preceded by other Maine vessels seeking to swap lumber for molasses, and any hope of getting 100 gallons for each 1,000 board feet was ridiculous. From Port-au-Prince he went to St. Marks, and then back to Jérémie. He stayed there for 28 days trying to haggle for his gallon per ten board feet, but failing in this he decided to call it quits and take the best offer he could get. Since this was nowhere near what he had hoped for, he had space left for some coffee. He waited several weeks for this, and, finally, laden with molasses and coffee, he set sail for his beloved Maine.

If, and it is wildly possible, this were the vessel that gave Friendship her name, it certainly was before this tedious voyage. Because that *Friendship* was not one of the *Friendships* that came home. Two days at sea, Captain Wells lost both his ship and cargo.

But if anyone asks why Meduncook became Friendship—at least you can offer a few words.

IV

THE ORIGIN OF FRIENDSHIPS

by Malcolm Barter

Geography often determines how the people of a town make their living. Friendship is a good example. While farming, raising chickens and cutting granite all have had their day in Friendship, the sea that surrounds the town has been the principal source of income for as long as the town has existed. Since the first settlement early in the 18th century, residents have turned to clamming, lobstering and fishing of all sorts for their livelihood. The Indians who lived in the area long before the white man also relied on the sea for much of their subsistence.

The year 1880 was the high point in the population of the town of Friendship. In that year's census, 938 residents were registered, 253 of them males old enough to vote. Bremen, across the head of Muscongus Bay, reached its population zenith two decades earlier in 1860, with 908 people. Those were bustling, busy times that were never again equalled.

The monumental Fishery Commission report of 1887 provides considerable insight into the nature of the individuals represented in these census reports. While noting the insularity and cantankerousness of Maine fishermen in general —they wouldn't row the Commission's investigator "from place to place and thereby earn good wages, though many of them were doing nothing"—the report praised their eagerness to

"adopt inventions and discoveries that may promise to benefit them in their work."

Their work was fishing. In 1880, there were 8,100 men in the State of Maine engaged in fishing for their livelihood. Of this number, perhaps close to 1,000 made their homes along the shores and on the islands of Muscongus Bay, principally in the towns of Friendship, Bremen and Bristol. The Fisheries Commission reported that the majority married young and raised large families; lived in modest houses surrounded by a "patch" of ground on which they grew a few vegetables to supplement their diet of fish, lobsters and clams; and earned on the average, if fish were plentiful and bait not scarce, somewhere between $100 and $175 a year.

For the most part, they were self-employed in the inshore fisheries—lobstering, seining and hand-lining from small sloops in the Bay—but many also tried their hand at offshore fishing on Jeffrey's and Cashes Banks, and even on the Grand Banks off Newfoundland. When Gloucester fishing boat owners sought crews to man their schooners to the Banks, especially in the wintertime, they first tried to sign on "natives of Maine," who were "second to none in bravery, hardihood, and seamanship." Some fall or winter, if the fishermen of Muscongus Bay chanced not to be "getting up a boat," they

"Getting the boat afloat once it was finished apparently was a minor concern that was accomplished with good tackles, horses or oxen, and many willing hands."

made a trip or two from Gloucester. Often, too, they sailed to Gloucester and Boston in their own sloops and small schooners to sell catches of lobsters and fish.

To follow this way of life, boatbuilding was a necessity, and Friendship and the surrounding area produced their share of master boatbuilders. It is, of course, impossible to know every man who built a Friendhip Sloop, but it is safe to say that most every fisherman in the area in the late 1800's either built a boat or helped with the building of one. Dories, skiffs, centerboard sloops, and schooners, as well as Friendship Sloops, were constructed along every shore.

Outside of Wilbur Morse, who built Sloops in mass production, turning out sometimes as many as two every three months with the help of a large crew of workers, builders worked largely alone. A man would build a boat during the winter to use for fishing all summer. Then in the fall, he would sell the sloop and build another the next winter. This would provide next summer's fishing boat, a little revenue, and work for the winter.

All the wood for these boats was cut on the mainland. Each man cut his own red oak and white pine, and usually hauled it to the sawmill at Bristol Mills. The sawmill was open at both ends so a team of horses could haul the logs right into the mill to unload. Then came the problem of getting the long pieces of lumber over to the island. This was accomplished by stretching the planks across two dories and thus floating the load to the island.

The site for building a boat often was not chosen for its accessibility to the water, but because it provided the most convenient shelter, even if it chanced to be the third floor of a fish house or the loft of a barn, perhaps miles from the sea. Getting the boat afloat once it was finished apparently was a minor concern that was accomplished with good tackles, horses or oxen, and many willing hands. Some boats were even hauled onto the ice and left there to launch themselves when the ice thawed.

Everyone in the community had a part in the construction of the "sloop-boats." Women sewed sails by the hour, while the men toiled at steaming timbers and carefully fitting on the planks. Children eagerly looked forward to the launching day. On that great occasion, Clifford Winchenbach's daughter recalls with exhilara-

Courtesy, Red Boutilier

" 'The centerboarder remained popular into the early 1890's . . . ' " (This is the 32-foot Muscongus Bay Sloop, *Sopolio*, built on Bremen Long Island in the late 1800's by Abdon Carter. Verne Carter, the son of her owner, Albion M. Carter, still has the cup she won in the Round Pound Yacht Race of July 4th, 1894.)

tion, everyone came from near and far to help or just to watch. " 'Cliffy' would supply the honey, and we all had a 'bee.' "

It is easy to see how the Friendship Sloop was named: so many of them were built at Friendship or nearby. It is not so easy to discover exactly how the design originated.

Some say Wilbur Morse dreamed up the design while lying in his bunk on a Gloucester schooner after a hard day's fishing on the Grand Banks. Others claim that some of Wilbur's neighbors on Bremen Long Island—the Mc-Lains, and Carters and the Collamores—were in Gloucester one day and saw a Gloucester sloop boat aground. Having been beaten in races to market by some of these craft, the story goes, they decided to see what made them sail so fast. They took note of the smoothly planked hull, the full mid-section, and deep keel—all in

contrast with the lapstreaked, much less powerful, shallow centerboard sloops most of them were using back home on Muscongus Bay.

Howard Chapelle, on the other hand, suggests it was not so much Wilbur Morse's "dreaming" or "stealing off the lines" by his fellow Bremen Long Islanders that produced the Friendship Sloop.

He wrote as follows in his book, *American Small Sailing Craft*:

"The centerboarder remained popular into the early 1890's; by that time it was rapidly being replaced by a keel hull of the same rig and general appearance. The records are not clear as to why this occurred but indicate that the centerboard sloop had been ousting the Casco Bay Hampton boat type in the vicinity of Muscongus Bay. This seems to have begun as early as 1885, and by 1890, or thereabouts, the Mon-

One of the old single-headsail Sloops used in Muscongus Bay in the 1870's and 1880's.

hegan and Matinicus boats were quite out of fashion there. The centerboard sloop had a rather short reign and was soon being replaced by the keel model.

"The keel lobster sloop did not represent an innovation, of course. The Muscongus Bay builders had turned out keel fishing sloops as early as 1850, and their craft followed the trend in design that existed in the Gloucester sloop-boats. In the late 1870's and early 80's, the then popular model of fishing schooner, a shoal and very sharp keel boat, came under violent criticism as the cause of much loss of life. As a result, new schooners were built in the early 80's of greater depth in proportion to beam and

A working Friendship at rest. The *Elvia Alice*.

The *Siren II* was owned by Ed Leeman of Round Pound, Maine. She used to sail fishing parties out of Damariscotta.

length; this set up a new trend in design that shortly affected the sloops. It seems very probable that this change in fashion was felt in Muscongus Bay, and the fishermen now wanted a deeper boat in place of the older centerboarder. The keel sloop of the present Friendship sloop style of hull and rig certainly appeared late in the 1880's, and this model was shortly a very popular one among the lobstermen. The sloops also grew in size, and gaff topsails soon appeared. The old "jumbo" headsail of the fishing schooner had just gone out of style, and the double-headsail rig was now the rage. So the lobster sloops had double headsails in the place of the old single jib. These additions and changes did not occur as a result of trial of the comparative merits of the old and the new, but were the result of a fad for a given hull and rig form that was being created by publicity in behalf of a safer fishing schooner."

The "new" Friendship Sloop was readily accepted. As soon as it had proved itself among the ledges of Muscongus Bay and had soundly beaten sloops from Rockland in several races, demand for these boats spread up and down the coast.

A leading family of builders of Friendship Sloops was the Morses. Grandpa Jonah passed on to his sons Albion, Charles, Wilbur and Jonah, the great art of boatbuilding. Albion moved to Pleasant Point, Cushing, where he is reported to have built nearly 100 Sloops. Charles built boats in Friendship before moving to Thomaston to what is still known as the Morse Boat Yard. Wilbur, having built his first Sloop at the age of 19, set up his first shop about two miles from the water. Nine years later, he moved to Friendship Harbor. When he was 19 too, young Jonah went to work for his older brother Wilbur, and it was not long before the two formed a partnership that lasted some 35 years.

Bremen Long Island was also a lively boat-building community, with boat shops dotting the shore. Neighbors, fathers, sons and brothers built Sloops side by side. There was George Washington (Wash) Carter, and his sons George, Norris and Abdon. Abdon built the *Florida*, from which the famous *Pemaquid* lines were taken. Robert A. McLain, builder of the *Estella A*, on display at the Mystic Seaport and now being rebuilt in Thomaston, was building Friendship Sloops along with his sons, Robert E., Eugene, Almond and Alexander. Charles Carter, Vincent Collamore, William Prior, and George Prior were also active Sloop builders. In the year 1900 alone, builders on Bremen Long Island launched 22 Friendship Sloops.

Most of the young men learned how to build Sloops from the older generation. Charles Carter was the exception. When he asked his uncle how to plank his Sloop, the reply was, "Charles, you plank 'er yourself, and you'll never have to ask anyone how to do it again."

Through their genius as boatbuilders, these men provided the fishermen of their era a boat they could afford and, above all, one that was able and handy. They knew she would take them out and they knew she would bring them back—the Friendship Sloop.

V

FRIENDSHIPS IN TRANSITION

by AL ROBERTS

The Friendship Sloop was designed and used as a fishing boat, and primarily as a lobster fishing boat. When gasoline engines began to replace sails, the lobster fishermen of Maine were slow to accept the change. Friendship Sloops had served them well for nearly three decades, but slowly they began to realize that tradition was one thing, and competition and efficiency were another. By 1915, the gasoline engine appeared to be here to stay, and the boatyards building Friendship Sloops were forced into building power boats. The evolution of the lobster boat is a story in itself, and the only mention we will make of it here is to note that from Sloops, the lobster boats went to double enders, acorn sterns, narrow transom sterns, and gradually wider and wider transom sterns, until today the stern of a lobster boat is only slightly less wide than the greatest beam amidships.

During the 30 years prior to 1915, there were so many Friendship Sloops built in the Muscongus Bay area there could be no way of estimating the number, but it would be safe to guess it was well over a thousand. From 1925 to the inception of the Friendship Sloop Society in 1961, there were no more than a half dozen Sloops built commercially and perhaps another half dozen by backyard boatbuilders who wanted one for themselves.

During the thirties and forties, Warren Prescott Gannett's yard in Scituate, Massachusetts, built a few Friendship Sloops. We know about five of these:

Old Friendly—built in 1938, a 24-footer, now owned by Donald Hall of Amherst, Massachusetts.

Retriever—built in 1942, a 22-footer, now owned by John Rice of Scituate, Massachusetts.

Pal-o-mine—a 27-footer, built in 1947, now owned by James Lane of Winchester, Massachusetts.

Bounty—date of launching unknown, a 23-foot Sloop, owned by Dr. Roy Gumpel of Rye, New York.

Surprise—(not to be confused with Phil Nichols' *Surprise*). The history of this Sloop has been lost.

The first four of these have been classified as Class B Sloops (following the lines of the original Sloops and built since 1921) by the Society, and it is assumed the fifth may well have been a Class B type also.

Winfield Scott Carter of Friendship, a descendant of the Carters who built Friendship Sloops on Bremen Long Island, built three Friendships in three years during this period. In 1936, he built a 30-footer that was named the *Flying Jib* at her launching, then became

Irving Nevells

"Murray Peterson, who has designed the famous yacht replicas of coasting schooners, has designed two Sloops and both are beautiful boats, particularly with their topsails set. Roger Duncan's *Eastward* (opposite page) is one, and the *Heritage*, owned by William Hadlock of South Freeport, Maine, is the other."

Monique and is now known as the *Flying Jib* again. She is owned by Newton Hinckley of Wayland, Massachusetts. Scott's second Friendship was the *Tannis II*, now owned by John Cronin of Sturbridge, Massachusetts. The *Tannis II* is a 38-foot Sloop, built in 1937. In 1938, Scott built his third sloop, *Eleazar*, a 38-foot boat. She was later sold to a Mr. Shelhorn, then in turn to Carl Arra of Newburg, New York, and finally to Harold Marden of Wilmington, Delaware, the present owner, who renamed her the *Gold Ivy*.

Carlton Simmons, while he was Postmaster of Friendship, built a 30-foot sloop in 1945 in the barn behind the post office. She was for Robert Armstrong, Sr. of Winchester, Massachusetts, a long time summer resident of Friendship.. This Sloop was later used by John Armstrong, a son of Robert, and Franklin Perkins, Jr., as a party boat during the summer months. She sailed out of Perkins Cove in Ogunquit. She also cruised to the Bahamas. Franklin Perkins now is the proud owner of the smallest Sloop ever to sail in the Regatta, the *Departure*, a Class C boat, (a replica that deviates slightly from the original lines), of only 15 feet. The first year she raced, she towed a dory all the way from Ogunquit that was longer than she was! It is reported that when she first sailed into Perkins Cove, an old timer was heard to remark, "Well I'll be—a Friendship cat finally had a kitten!"

Carlton Simmons comes by his boatbuilding

ability and enthusiasm naturally, as he is a grand nephew of Wilbur Morse. In 1963, Carlton decided to build himself a Sloop. He finally settled on a 26-foot gaff-rigged Sloop, reminiscent of a Friendship, but by the time he got around to the planking stage he sold her to John Hennings of Falmouth, Maine, who finished her. In 1968, Kenneth Billings of Manchester, Massachusetts, bought her. He has renamed her the *Pam*.

In 1956 and 1958 there were two Friendships built. One by James Chadwick, for Roger and Mary Duncan of West Concord, Massachusetts, and Newagen, Maine, and the other by Lash Brothers of Friendship, Maine, for John Dallett of New York City. Mr. Dallett has recently sold his 30-footer, the *Mary Anne* to Dr. Joe Griffin of Damariscotta, Maine, and Roger and Mary Duncan sail parties out of Newagen during the summer months in their 32-foot *Eastward*. The Lash Brothers, Doug and Winnie, are related to old time Sloop builders on both sides of their family, on one side to the Carters and on the other to the McLains. Who says shipbuilding ability is not inherited?

Another builder, related directly to the old time Friendship builders, is Roger Morse, of the Morse boatbuilding yard in Thomaston, Maine. Roger is a direct descendant of all the famous Morse boatbuilders. Roger's father was Charles. The Morse yard built the *Sadie M* for Harrison Prindle of Bethesda, Maryland, and Castine, Maine, in 1946. In 1968, Mr. Prindle added the clipper bow which she lacked, and in 1969 he sold her to Robert Emerson of Hancock Point, Maine, who renamed her the *Vigor*.

The transition from work boats to yachts took 40 years, and culminated in 1961 with the establishment of a Society dedicated to reviving the venerable Friendship to make the boating public fully aware of her potential as a family sailing yacht. Everyone who had ever seen one admired them, but now suddenly everyone wanted one. The demand was estab-

Elmer Barde

lished. Someone had to get busy to meet the demand.

The Lash Brothers of Friendship had built the *Mary Anne* just three years previously, so they were ready and willing to get into production using plans they had inherited from their forebears. Roger Morse still had old plans, and the Newbert and Wallace yard in Thomaston had access to plans through an employee, Arthur McFarland of Friendship. Arthur's mother was step-daughter to Jonah Morse, and Jonah was foreman of his brother Wilbur's boatyard for years. The plans Arthur had are reportedly those drawn on a brown paper bag and handed down from Jonah.

As word spread about the revival of the Friendships, interest seemed to be generated everywhere at once. Letters poured in asking for details, for plans, for names of Sloops for sale, for names of builders, and architects. Howard Chapelle's office at the Smithsonian Institution in Washington, D.C., was swamped with letters of inquiry, and the W. W. Norton Publishing Company did a land office business in plans for the *Pemaquid* (of which more in the next chapter). The availability of plans made the *Pemaquid* a popular model, because other plans were extremely difficult to come by.

One letter received by the Secretary of the Friendship Sloop Society was from James Rockefeller of Camden, Maine, who professed to be interested in traditional boats, and expressed a desire to build at least one Friendship Sloop on speculation, out of pure love for the design. Jim's boatyard sits atop Bald Mountain in Camden—as unlikely a spot for a boatyard as you could find—but Jim has built two beautiful Friendships, completely rebuilt another, and has even finished off a couple of fiberglass Friendship hulls. As this goes to press, Jim has orders for another wooden Friendship and has another fiberglass hull to be finished. Dr. A. Carl Maier of Mayfield Heights, Ohio, has contracted with Jim for the construction of the wooden

sloop, and Ebenezar Gay of Hingham, Massachusetts, is going to have the fiberglass model.

The first Sloop to be built at Jim's Bald Mountain Boat Works was hauled to the sea by two yoke of oxen over a distance of nearly eight miles. It was quite a sight to see a Friendship Sloop being hauled in such a traditional manner. Once at the water's edge the tradition ended, for who ever heard of a Friendship being launched via a Travelift?

Murray Peterson, who has designed the famous yacht replicas of coasting schooners, has designed two Sloops, and both are beautiful boats, particularly with their topsails set. Roger Duncan's *Eastward* is one, and the *Heritage*, owned by William Hadlock of South Freeport, Maine, is the other. The *Heritage* is 29 feet long.

Perhaps the most expensive Sloop built was to the specifications of Joseph Plumb of Rochester, Massachusetts, at the Simms yard in Scituate, Massachusetts. Rumor has it that the *Dottie G.* cost over $30,000 or $1,000 per foot. Teak, African mahogany, bronze, stainless steel, Monel, gold leaf—all this is a far cry from the pine, oak, and galvanized fastenings of the good old days, when a Sloop all set to sail away sold for $450.00. (See plans at back of book.)

McKie Roth built the *Galatea*, which currently graces the harbor of San Francisco. Nick Roth came to Maine and talked to the descendants of early builders, and went back to California to try to produce a true Friendship. Finally New England and the Sloops "got to him" so much that he sold out his boat yard there, and moved to Maine where he set up his present shop in North Edgecomb. In this past year, he has turned out two pretty little Sloops: the *Philia* for Bruce Myers of MacMahan Island, Maine, and the *Eagle* for Colonel Philip Groetzinger of Wiscasset, Maine. He is working on two more Sloops on order.

There are many more modern-day builders.

34

Tom Jones

"Nick Roth . . . moved to Maine where he set up his present shop in North Edgecomb. In this past year, he has turned out . . . the *Eagle* for Colonel Philip Groetzinger of Wiscasset, Maine."

Some are individuals, such as Malcolm Brewer and Philip Nichols, who are constructing on speculation, some are boatyards building on order, and there are many people building their own Sloops in barns, garages, and back yards.

Nor is this love of a Friendship Sloop confined to the United States. The Admiral's Inn at English Harbor, Antigua, boasts a Friendship burgee hanging alongside the pennants of yacht clubs from around the world, and an Englishman, Eric Osborn, will fly the British ensign on his Friendship Sloop, the *Yankee Trader*. An American, seeking a boat for his family, consulted a Danish yard, and was told to look at a Friendship Sloop before he made up his mind what type boat he wanted.

Some hard-working, time-bothered, would-be Sloop owners have turned to fiberglass and also ferro-cement construction. The fewer maintenance hours allow these people to enjoy their leisure days sailing, without spending tedious and hard-to-come-by time sanding and painting.

Until recently, the thought of a fiberglass

35

Friendship Sloop brought a reaction as if to heresy from died-in-the-wool enthusiasts. But the up-lifted arms have fallen, the dropped jaws have closed, the bulged eyes receded, and the Friendship Sloop Society and ardent traditionalists have accepted the word "fiberglass" in connection with Friendship Sloops. To quote Jim Rockefeller: "Boats are for fun. What difference if they are built of wood, cement, glass, or melted down old chocolate-covered rubber heels, long as the material is used well and honestly and the result is pleasing to the eye and it does the job."

It was inevitable that the fiberglass Friendship would come about, just as it was inevitable man would stand on the moon. You can't stop progress. The Friendship Sloop itself answered a need of the fishermen, and now the new fiberglass answers the need of the busy man who wants to sail, but has no time for maintaining his boat.

The first application for membership in the Friendship Sloop Society of a fiberglass Friendship reached the Society during the summer of 1969. Bruno and Stillman had constructed a 30-foot fiberglass Friendship for Harold E. Kimball, and he wanted to race his *Perseverance* in the Regatta. Jarvis Newman had a 25-foot fiberglass Sloop, the *Salatia*, most completed, and he wanted to bring her to Friendship. Thus at the Skipper's Meeting that summer, it was voted to welcome our glass friends to the Society. However, because we do not know how the fiberglass and wooden Sloops will race, boat for boat, a new class, Class D, was established for other than wooden Sloops. Until there has been time enough to evaluate any differences the wooden and fiberglass Sloops will race together, but for separate trophies.

The Society at this writing knows of only three boatyards engaged in constructing fiberglass Friendship Sloop hulls: Jarvis Newman in Southwest Harbor, Maine, is building a 25-foot Sloop; Bruno and Stillman in Newington,

New Hampshire, has a 30-foot boat; and the Passamaquoddy Yacht Company at Medfield, Massachusetts, is working on a 22-footer.

About everyone interested in boats has visited a yard sometime and has witnessed some or all stages of building a wooden boat. There is the laying of the keel, bending timbers, planking, and all the familiar procedures. Very few laymen have much idea about making a fiberglass boat. First, a mold has to be constructed, or if an existing boat is used, she has to have all exterior hardware, trim, and paint removed. The hull mold is then put on its side and the new fiberglass hull mold made one half at a time. Following this the deck mold is made.

One builder uses a minimum of one-half inch thickness of fiberglass throughout the hull, with the keel area having from two to five inches. The deck is also one-half inch thick. The lead keel is bonded to the hull.

Reports have reached us of two ferro-cement Friendship Sloops that have already been constructed. The Society will welcome them all, be they fibergass, ferro-cement, or "chocolate covered rubber heels."

The attitude of most present-day owners toward their Friendship Sloops is summed up by a remark of a past president of the Society. "The Friendship Sloop is more than a boat—she is a state of mind as well."

VI

BUILDING FRIENDSHIPS

by AL ROBERTS and EDWARD W. COFFIN

The "do-it-yourself" craze that swept the country a few years ago invaded the boating field, and so it was inevitable there would be people trying to build Friendship Sloops in their back yards, or garages, or barns, or wherever. Despite advice from the "old timers" that there is no boat more difficult to build than a Friendship, and that only experienced hands should attempt such an undertaking, there have been many Friendships successfully completed at the hands of amateurs.

If all the Sloops were built in reality that are conceived in the dreams of sailors the world over, there wouldn't be room in the oceans for anything else. The mail received by Betty Roberts, our Secretary, contains a couple of letters every week from people inquiring about the availablity of plans for Friendship Sloops. These letters come from about every state in the Union, and from such places as Japan, England, and Taiwan.

The old saying that a boat builder can build a house, but a house carpenter can't built a boat, does not seem to apply when the carpenter is motivated by his love for the traditional and beautiful lines of a Friendship Sloop.

Two of the prettiest little Sloops to participate in the Regatta in Friendship, are the *Content* and the *Ellie T*, built by Stuart Ford and John Thorpe respectively. "Stu" Ford was retired and well into his seventies when be built the *Content* almost single-handed over a three-year period. John Thorpe was a working man who had the help of his wife, Eleanore, for whom the Sloop was named, and his three young children, Katy, Henry, and John, Jr. John estimated there were 3,000 hours of work put into the *Ellie T*, but they were hit-or-miss hours—one today, two yesterday—and an occasional week-end or two. This is not a very efficient way to work, but one that gives much pleasure when your heart is all wrapped up in it, as John's was—and the end result becomes one of the family.

Because of the availability of the plans for the well-known 25-foot *Pemaquid*, most of the do-it-yourselfers have used this design. These plans were made available by the W. W. Norton Publishing Company in New York City after they were used to illustrate the section on Friendship Sloops in Howard Chapelle's book *American Small Sailing Craft*. The original name of the *Pemaquid* was *Florida*. She was built in 1914 by Abdon Carter of Bremen, Maine. In 1922, Willard Thorpe of Christmas Cove, Maine, father of the aforementioned John Thorpe, bought the *Florida* from Randall Simmons of Loud's Island. The next owner,

Andrew Hepburn renamed her *Pemaquid*. The late Charles MacGregor, of Lynn, Massachusetts, took off her lines, and it was these lines that Howard Chapelle used in his book. Both "Stu" Ford and John Thorpe call another of Chapelle's books, *Boatbuilding*, their guiding light or "Bible" and admit that without his help the building of their Sloops would have been impossible.

Reginald Wilcox of Boothbay, Maine, is another Friendship enthusiast who built his own Sloop with no previous experience. "Reg" did it the hard way, even to sawing out the 31-foot, 29-inch keel by hand, a task that took 48 working hours. The launching of the *Emmie B* was in 1958. He had started construction in 1951. It's not a bit uncommon for a "do-it-yourself" Sloop builder to take many years to complete his work. It's not quite clear whether or not they prolong the work purposely because it is a labor of love.

Phil Nichols, of Round Pond, Maine, spent nine years of tender loving care in the building of his 33-footer, the *Surprise*. Now at the age of 75, Phil is building his fourth Friendship, and there is much conjecture as to what Phil will name her. His first was the *Result*, a 28-footer; his second was the 37-foot *Pressure*; the *Surprise* was his third; and the Sloop now under construction is a smaller edition of the *Surprise*, which hopefully will be launched in 1970. We list Phil with the do-it-yourself builders, because even though he appears to be a bona-fide boat builder now, until his retirement Phil was a draftsman.

Kenneth Rich, of New London, New Hampshire, is building a *Pemaquid*, and Robert White of League City, Texas, is having trouble finding proper materials and fittings for his *Pemaquid* in what he calls "a fiberglass world." The pictures White has sent showing his Friendship in his backyard make one do a "double take," for overhanging her deck are the fronds of palm trees.

The *Lucy Anne* is another *Pemaquid*, this one built and owned by James Hall of Rowley, Massachusetts. She spends her winters in Round Pond, Maine.

The *Allegiance* is a brand new 24-footer, built by her owner, Albert Harding, of Kennebunkport, Maine.

We have no outstanding or noteworthy information about the building of many of these owner-built Sloops, but merely list them with the knowledge that many readers of this account will look up the builders to "talk shop," and there is not a more enjoyable pastime for any of these men.

Jeremy Maxwell of Spruce Head, Maine, and Nathaniel Clapp, of Prides Crossing, Massachusetts, are the only owner-builders we know of who have started construction in one state and transported the hull overland to be finished in another. Clapp built the hull of his tiny, 20-foot Friendship in Massachusetts and had her hauled to East Boothbay, Maine, where he had Goudy and Stevens do the rigging. She was named the *Mary C* and was launched from the Goudy and Stevens yard in 1962. Although marconi rigged, she is a beautifully traditional Sloop in every other detail. Jerry Maxwell's small, 21-footer has proved to be too small for cruising with four aboard, so Jerry has decided to build another Sloop with more room. No doubt this one will be finished where she's started, because Jerry is now a dyed-in-the-wood Mainiac, and is not about to cross a state border in mid-construction on this one as he did with his *Tern*.

Ed Coffin, of Owls Head, Maine, is building a *Pemaquid*. We'll let him tell about that project himself.

AL ROBERTS

"We ordered her plans by Chapelle
from the W. W. Norton Publishing Company at a cost of $12."

"The red oak keel is 6 by 8 inches by
18 feet long and cost $25. (Jeff Coffin,
aged 10, cuts the rabbet, while Diana
Coffin, aged 5, gathers strength for future
efforts.)

RAY OF HOPE

I once read somewhere that rowing away
from your boat and looking back in pride at
your accomplishment of wood to water is the
height of love afloat. Naturally, this point of
view is strongly shared by all dockside loafers.
As one of Maine's leading dockside loafers, my
appetite always becomes strangely full when
viewing the gaff rig and the powerful sheer of
a Friendship Sloop. This always led to a fierce
desire, which, in my case, started to slacken
when we began to build a replica of the famous
25-foot *Pemaquid*.

We ordered her plans by Chapelle from the
W. W. Norton Publishing Company at a cost
of $12. Our boat shop on western Penobscot
Bay, where we are building, measures 38x22x12
feet, with windows on the whole east and south
walls. It is a grand building in which to build
small craft. From the 25-foot-long workbench,
one can see Heron Neck Light, on Vinalhaven,
and the outer ledges and islands of the Muscle
Ridge Channel, where the Friendship Sloops
long ago used to earn their keep.

For earlier boat building projects before our
shop was built, we used a friend's barn floor
for lofting lines and built outdoors in a pole
shed made of scrap boards covered with tarpaper and canvas and open on the north side.

"Now that the backbone was up and trued to a center line, the molds were placed on station from the plans and braced off from the shop roof and walls." (Diana Coffin, ready to go to work.)

Our biggest incentive for building the *Pemaquid* model came from a friendly duck hunter, who, having built one for himself, offered me an extra cast iron keel of 2,000 pounds for $352. It came with eight hull molds and patterns.

The planking of native one-inch cedar was ordered first, to allow for drying time. It cost $138 for 950 feet, of which 250 feet was an inch-and-a-quarter thick for planking around

the turn of the bilge where you have to hollow out to fit the curve of the frames. This amount of planking allows for numerous mistakes.

I would have liked to use galvanized nails for planking, but the friendly duck hunter insisted I use Everdur screws. "You will have potential buyers visit with you longer that way," he said. It has taken 20 gross of inch-and-a-half by No. 12 screws for planking. This cost $99.

I drew out to full size on the shop floor the

Edward W. Coffin

"Two of the most difficult areas of construction that caused strain in my brain were: one, the curved transom with its quarterblocks, and, two, the proper cutting of the changing angle of the stern deadwood rabbet."

"The transom of the *Pemaquid* model is of handsome line and, if properly executed, is a beautifying complement to the whole boat."

"The molds being in position and the rabbets roughed out, we were ready for the spruce ribbands to be sprung around the molds to hold the shape rigid."

shape of the keel and all the deadwood. This controlled the fit of the wood to the tapered iron keel and gave me two sore knees! The red oak keel is 6 by 8 inches by 18 feet long and cost $25. This is the same good Maine red oak used in yacht and fishing dragger construction and by all lobster pot builders. Contrary to popular thinking, many knowledgeable marine architects hold it in high regard.

The deadwood and keel bolts are three-quarter-inch galvanized iron and were found in a local junkyard. With threading and fitted with washers and nuts, they came to $27.

Once the oak backbone was fitted and sized and the rabbet cut, the whole assembly was treated for about a week to a daily brushing of a mixture composed of half linseed oil and half turpentine, to prevent checking of the backbone and deadwood. The oak keel, to be bolted to the iron keel, was first redleaded on the bottom and a 30-pound-weight sheet of tarpaper fitted in between to insulate the oak from the iron keel. After the backbone was blocked up and plumbed to grade, a hole was bored two inches deep or more in the stemtop. A funnel was inserted into which was poured the turps and linseed mixture until it ran out the bottom of the stem, showing full saturation. This is necessary in a warm shop, as the wet oak when drying out would pull off line and crack.

Now that the backbone was up and trued to a center line, the molds were placed on station from the plan and braced off from the shop roof and walls. At this point of construction I would suggest that every night before turning in, in addition to reading the Bible, the amateur boatbuilder read Chapelle's book on boatbuilding. This volume will give good

Edward W. Coffin

" 'T is a wonderful thing to have a sympathetic helper. Francis Nash, my superintendent of the Tug and Grunt Boatyard and only employee, is my third arm. He provided the incentive for much of the difficult work on this boat."

"As of March 1970, the Sloop was two years under construction and was all planked with the clamp and shelf in."

Edward W. Coffin

simple directions for tomorrow's step in assembling the "ark."

Two of the most difficult areas of construction that caused strain in my brain were: one, the curved transom with its quarterblocks, and, two, the proper cutting of the changing angle of the stern deadwood rabbet. I was fortunate in being able to visit Sloops under construction in the area and to see how professionals handled these sections. I found that all were most willing to help me when in trouble with a difficult task. Never hesitate to ask advice.

The transom of the *Pemaquid* model is of handsome line and, if properly executed, is a beautifying complement to the whole boat. It was laid out of one-and-three-quarters-by-five-inch oak on a curved rack built up of two-by-eigth-inch spruce to hold the boiled oak transom frame to shape. Once assembled, the transom was bolted to the horn timber with a knee.

The molds being in position and the rabbets roughed out, we were ready for the spruce ribbands to be sprung around the molds to hold the shape rigid. Once they were nailed in position and braced off from the floor, we then turned to fashioning the one-by-two-inch frames.

The oak frames were cut from a flat grain; they cost $30. These were placed eight at a time, in a mixture of one gallon of permanent anti-freeze and a quantity of water and were boiled for about 30 minutes, or until pliable. The anti-freeze additive, for some reason, leaves the frames a natural color, whereas boiled water will usually turn oak black. The boiling tank was built of two old galvanized hot water tanks, which were found on the local dump. They were welded together with a supporting frame fixed to the front end so as to allow a fire of scrapwood to be built beneath. It took

"Looking back at the time spent working on the boat—weekends and some weekdays—we found ourselves tentatively drawing a name on the handsome transom: *Ray of Hope!*"

almost two days to frame the boat. Why hurry what should be an enjoyable process?

'T is a wonderful thing to have a sympathetic helper. Francis Nash, my superintendent of the Tug and Grunt Boat Yard and only employee, is my third arm. He provided the incentive for much of the difficult work on this boat. When a wrong cut was made, or a piece fitted poorly, his well-chosen comments gave new hope. I recall how I ruined part of the stern deadwood early in the job and Nash's comment was, "Never mind, there is plenty of wood still growing in the forest. Let's go get us another chunk."

One of the greatest contributions by the plastics industry to wooden boat builders is the new blue car body putty. This costs about $1.80 per quart and may be obtained in an auto store. But if you buy it from a marine shop, the same thing costs $8.00. This putty sets up like iron and is workable by file or plane. Using this on many holes and voids I found gave one the feeling of being a sculptor. This thought can become rather dangerous, if you start thinking, "Maybe I can build the whole boat of blue putty and just use wood for fuel in the stove."

As of March, 1970, the Sloop was two years under construction and was all planked with the clamp and shelf in. Looking back at the time spent working on the boat—weekends and some weekdays—we found ourselves tentatively drawing a name on the handsome transom: *Ray of Hope!* This will not necessarily be the final name, but it reflects the attitude of the builder and his family. The cost that we see to date is about $1,200.

We amateur boat builders are like good English tea—our strength really shows when we get in hot water.

EDWARD W. COFFIN.

VII

PRESERVING A FRIENDSHIP

by Al Roberts

Newell McLain is the son of R. E. McLain, Jr., master boatbuilder, and was born on Bremen Long Island in 1895. He remembers well many of the Friendship Sloop launchings, but one he recalls particularly well is that of the *Estella A* in 1904. (See plans at back of book.)

The *Estella A* is the Sloop that for many years has held a prominent berth at the Mystic Seaport, Mystic, Connecticut. She is now being overhauled at the Newbert and Wallace yard in Thomaston, Maine, just a long stone's throw from Newell's front door on Thatcher Street. As a boy Newell watched her being launched from a front window in his home on Bremen Long Island, and now in two minutes he can walk to the yard to watch the progress of her rejuvenation. It would seem safe to say he will be at her re-launching when once more she takes the water to sail back to the Mystic Seaport. This will undoubtedly make him the only person to have been present at both launchings.

Back in her native state for much-needed repairs, the *Estella A* is to get an extensive face lifting that will bring her back to her original condition insofar as is possible. She is 34.5 feet long, with a beam of 11.8 feet and a draft of 5.7 feet. She was the first Friendship to be launched on Bremen Long Island with auxiliary power, and if she was not the very first auxiliary

in the area, then she was one of the first. She had a 9-h.p., 2-cylinder Knox engine with a clutch and reverse gear (the Knox engines were built in nearby Rockland, Maine). Her original ballast was all inside and consisted of pig iron instead of the rocks so commonly used at that time.

She was built for Jack Ames of Matinicus. When Jack contracted with "Rob" McLain to have her built, the price was set at $425.00, with the stipulation that if she was completed by March 1st, there would be a $25.00 bonus. To help meet this deadline, Rob hired Steve Prior to help, and the March 1st date was met in spite of complications due to cold weather.

The winter of 1904 was severe, and the ice was thicker and stronger than usual. Newell McLain recalls there was 22 inches of ice in the channel and up to 8 inches all the way to "Ruth's Nubble," a mile downstream. A channel was cut in the ice to a point below low water mark, and the launching went off without a hitch. The shears used to step the mast were set up on the ice, and she was rigged right where she sat, completely frozen in.

On the delivery date, Ed Poland, in his steam-driven lobster smack came up river to free the *Estella A* from her icy prison, and encountered more ice than he could handle,

"The *Estella A* is the Sloop that for many years has held a prominent berth at the Mystic Seaport, Mystic, Connecticut."

even with his ice plow in place. With much shuddering and screeching and banging, the best he could do with a running start, was to put the *Lucretia* into the ice about half her length. Before the day was over, there were more than a hundred men sawing ice and "tucking" the cakes under the solid ice. A channel over a mile long had to be cleared so the *Lucretia* could tow the *Estella A* clear of the ice and off to Matinicus.

Newell McLain recalls there were no "screw bolts" used in her construction below deck. All the iron was "driven iron," headed over with a mall and driven home. The above-deck hardware was much more rugged than is used today.

The bolts were forged and the nuts "blacksmith tapped" (one-sixteenth-inch larger than the bolt). Everything was sent to Bath for retapping and galvanizing and was freighted back to the island again. The cost for all the hardware on the Sloop, the galvanizing, and the freight came to $8.50. At today's prices the freight bill alone would be more than double that.

With such costs, $450.00 seems a reasonable price for a 34-foot auxiliary sloop delivered on time. Newell recalls how his father, Rob McLain, built a 26-foot Sloop for Martin Willey and cleared $60.00 for a job that began in November and took until the first of June. When the final bill is in for the repairs to the

48

Estella A, it will undoubtedly be more than twenty times the original cost of the Sloop if all the work is done that needs doing.

For five years, the *Estella A* was a frieght carrier; between 1930 and 1935 she was used in the coasting trade. Then she became a yacht, and eventually wound up at Mystic.

Her deep, non-self-bailing cockpit was designed to carry fish, and by using kid boards to section it off, it became ostensibly a fish hold. It had no seats. The cabin had two bunks forward and one aft to port, a stove with an oven facing inboard, and two lockers. Her present-day, off-center companionway may not be in its original location. She still steers with a tiller, and her rigging remains basically unchanged: two jibs and the main, with no topmast.

For years, the *Estella A* has been a major attraction at Mystic Seaport, and, after her refurbishing, she is bound to be a thing of beauty once more, recalling to the minds of many an era past. She is a nostalgic monument to a lost way of life.

VIII

COMPETING FRIENDSHIPS

by AL ROBERTS and CY HAMLIN

The first Friendship Sloop Regatta was a great success and everyone had a wonderful time. But the Society members who had made it happen wondered about the future. Where were we heading? Who was eligible and who was not? Who could best manage the race itself? Who could do the handicapping? Who would classify the Sloops?

That an answer to these last two questions in particular was needed became apparent as more and more Sloop owners sent in applications for membership and requested entry forms to race. Some of the applicants were definitely not Friendship Sloops. Some were definitely the old genuine, originals built around the turn of the century. Some were faithful replicas, and some were imitations worthy of consideration. Three classes were set up and were called Classes A, B, and C. Class A was for Sloops built prior to 1921. Class B was for Sloops built since 1921 and following strictly the lines of the original Sloops. Class C was for any replica that deviated slightly from the original lines. Later, a fourth class, Class D, was designated for Sloops with other than wooden hull construction.

Now all we had to do was set up a committee to assign each applicant to a class. For this purpose we were lucky enough to acquire the services of Howard Chapelle, Cy Hamlin,

Murray Peterson, and Bertram Snow. This committee proved to be able and willing, but the process was too cumbersome. By the time pictures and lines travelled to the desks of four men for consideration, time would run out, and race time would be upon us before a decision could be made. We soon came up with the idea of a committee of three of the skippers themselves to classify each new Sloop that joined the Society. This system seems to be working satisfactorily; at least the skippers will have only themselves to blame if someone winds up in the wrong class.

It is important that the classification be correct only because of the trophies and prizes awarded the winners. Although all the Sloops start together and race over the same course together, there are awards given for each class as well as one for the overall winner of each.

Class A trophies are:

Eda Lawry Trophy—awarded by Eda Lawry, granddaughter of Wilbur Morse, in memory of Wilbur. This was a three-legged trophy and was thus retired by the *Chrissy* when she won it the third time consecutively. Friends of Eda are perpetuating this trophy in her memory. This trophy is awarded the winner in the Saturday Race.

Mason Philip Smith

"To be sure, in the excitement of the races, everyone catches the fever . . . "

Jonah D. Morse Trophy—awarded for the over-all winner in Class A and given in memory of Jonah Morse, Wilbur's brother, by Jonah's two daughters, Bessie and Carrie McFarland.

Class B trophies are:

Lash Brothers Trophy—awarded for the winner in the Saturday Race. This is a three-legged trophy presented by the Lash Brothers Boatyard.

Anjacaa Trophy—awarded the over-all winner in Class B. This is a three-legged trophy presented by Nancy and Dick Watson.

Class C trophies are:

George B. Morrill Trophy—awarded the winner of the Saturday Race.

Palawan Trophy—awarded the over-all winner, and also a three-legged trophy.

The Friendship Sloop Society presents a trophy to each class for the winner on Thursday and Friday, and for second and third places on Saturday.

An over-all trophy is given to the Sloop that makes the highest number of points during the three-day Regatta. These points are figured: one point for finishing, one point for each boat beaten, and one-quarter point for winning.

Carlton Simmons

"The Sloop Regatta is not like a class-boat race in which every boat has the same dimensions, same weight, and same sail area."

In addition to the above trophies, we have the Governor's Trophy. It was first presented by Governor John Reed of Maine at our first race in 1961. It is a three-legged trophy and is awarded each year to the Class A or B Sloop with the highest number of points over-all. It has been won by *Voyager, Downeaster, Eastward, Dirigo, Rights of Man,* and *Eagle.*

In 1969, Seilers presented a trophy which will be awarded each year to the Sloop with the happiest, most friendly and unusual crew. This is called *Die echte Freundschaftlich Trophäe,* meaning the True Friendship Trophy.

At the 1970 Regatta there will be yet another trophy awarded, this one to the Sloop with the youngest crew member. This is being presented by the grandchildren of John Gould and will be known as the John Gould Trophy.

As the fiberglass Sloops will be allowed to race for the first time in 1970, they too will have trophies for their Class D. The Newman Trophy, a fiberglass half model, will be awarded the over-all winner, and the Bruno and Still-

man Trophy will be awarded for the winner of the Saturday Race.

The competitive spirit and desire to win is inherent in all of us to a greater or lesser degree, but it is conspicuous by its absence at the Sloop races. To be sure, in the excitement of the races, everyone catches the fever, and does everything in his power to cross the finish line first, but where else in a boat race would you hear one skipper say to another in a close situation, "Let me know when you're ready to come about and I'll give you room."

The Sloop Regatta is not like a class-boat race in which every boat has the same dimensions, same weight, and same sail area. The Sloops were all gaff-rigged and clipper bowed, and carried a jib and staysail, but their variances were enormous. They varied in length from 15 feet to 45 feet, and in beam from 5½ to 13½ feet. Their ballast ranged from rocks, cement, window weights, or axe heads in the bilges, to modern lead keels. Some of the Sloop owners had cut down the length of booms and

53

Bill Thon

Occasionally, during a race, one sees evidence of close Friendships.

gaffs to make their boats easier to handle, while others had the original huge mainsail, and had even added topsails.

The man who has handicapped these varied Sloops these past ten years is Cy Hamlin, Naval Architect. Year after year, the finish of the races has been amazingly close. After completing an afternoon of racing over a 12 or 15-mile course, many times the first Sloop to finish is less than a half hour ahead of the boat finishing thirtieth.

The following is an article that Cy wrote for our second book, *It's A Friendship*, and explains how the handicapping is accomplished for the Friendship Sloop Races.

AL ROBERTS

54

HANDICAPPING

"Yacht racing as a spectator sport has never had very broad popular appeal. True, there are classic contests such as the America's Cup series and the U. S.-Canadian Fishing Schooner Races, in which two craft race on an equal footing. But, by and large, watching a race between assorted sizes of yachts is an unexciting diversion even for those knowledgeable about handicapping rules. One reason is that the order of finishing usually has nothing to do with the order of placing, i.e. who gets the silverware. This peculiar situation arises from the handicapping systems developed over the past hundred years for evaluating the speed potentials of yachts of different sizes and types.

"Although sometimes mathemetically complicated, the handicapping, or rating, of yachts, on the basis of their speed potential is simple in principle. Generally speaking, a yacht will go faster if it is longer, lighter in weight, and has more sail area, than another yacht. These three factors—length, displacement (or weight), and sail area—are combined mathematically in different ways in different rules, but the relationships are essentially the same.

"The 'rating' of a boat, i.e. its speed coefficient as computed under any particular method of handicapping, is given in the form of a number. This number is not a dimension, although it generally is fairly close in value to the waterline length of the boat. For each rating coefficient there is a corresponding speed at which a boat of that rating will theoretically sail. A Table of Time Allowances lists the speed for each rating, expressed as the number of seconds in which a boat of each rating will sail one nautical mile under average conditions.

"In a conventional sailing race, the boat with the largest rating is the scratch boat, and its time allowance is the base against which the time allowances of all the other boats in the fleet are compared. The difference in allowed time between the scratch boat and any lower rating boat, multiplied by the number of miles in the race, is the time which the scratch boat must allow the lower rating boat.

"For example, if, in a race of 100 miles' length, the time allowance of the scratch boat is 600 seconds per mile (a speed of six knots), and that of a competitor is 620 seconds per mile, then the second boat must finish within 20 x 100, or 2,000, seconds after the scratch boat in order to win over her on corrected time.

"It can be seen that quite a while might elapse after the first boat has finished a race before the actual winner on corrected time can be ascertained. While this delay is hard enough on the competitors, who have at least some idea of where they lie in the fleet as to time allowances, for a spectator it can be completely mystifying, especially one who is unfamiliar with the principles of handicapping.

"In an effort to dispel this mystery for the spectators of the early Maine Retired Skippers Races, the boats were started on their handicaps. In other words, the boats were started one after the other, spaced out according to their time allowances. Although reasonably sound in principle, this system in practice placed a heavy burden on the race committee, involving some fast stopwatch work, and frenzied loading and firing of the starting cannon when several close-rating boats were sent on their way. Another, more serious, drawback of starting the boats on their handicaps was that a flat calm might prevail during the starting period, so that when a breeze did come in all the boats in effect started over again and together, with the handicaps nullified.

Downeaster trying to slip by to weather of *Mary Anne*.

"This was the background leading to the devising of a method of handicapping boats with respect to distance sailed, rather than to time. In other words, the course would be arranged so that the distances sailed by the boats would be inversely proportional to the time allowances. In our example above, for instance, for every 6.2 miles the larger boat was required to sail, her smaller competitor would sail 6.0 miles.

"In setting up a distance-handicapped race, a base course is selected which the lowest rating boat will be able to sail in a convenient period of time. (The lowest rating boat is, in effect, the scratch boat of the fleet.) Somewhere along this course, preferably near the middle, a handicap leg extending off to one side is laid out. Along this handicap leg, a buoy is set for each boat, the buoys being spaced according to one-half the computed handicap distances. Each boat must round its own buoy before starting back for the finish line. The beginning of the handicap leg is marked by one or two buoys called

"What did you do with all that breeze?"
the skippers ask their crews.

the "gate." The handicap leg should be located where wind and current conditions are as nearly constant along its length as possible.

"Handicapping on distance has been used by the Friendship Sloop Society for its annual regattas from the beginning and the system has worked well. Spectators in particular like it because the boats place as they finish, with no calculations or waiting required, and because the finish can be very exciting as several boats use up their handicaps and approach the finish line together. Competitors like it because everyone starts, and theoretically finishes, together, thus enjoying (or suffering) the same weather and current conditions. And the Race Committee (bless their hard working souls!) likes it because once the fleet is started, their work is practically done except to keep track of the order of finishing.

"The most exacting operation in this type of race is setting out the individual buoys along the handicap leg before the race. The buoy drops may be carefully timed in relation to the speed of the setting boat to achieve the correct spacing, or the individual position of each buoy may be determined by cross-bearings.

"During the three-day Friendship Sloop Regatta, the same course and handicap leg are used throughout. The first two days the contesting sloops merely sail around their own distinctively marked buoys and hurry back to the finish line. On the third day, however, the sloop crews are required to bring their buoys aboard, in simulation of hauling a lobster trap, this adding an extra demand on the skill of the skipper and crew and enhancing the excitement still further. (Editor's note: over the years, it has been found desirable to attach a light toggle to each handicap buoy by a light lanyard. The toggle bears the same number as the buoy to which it is attached. Each day the crew must snatch this toggle aboard and bring it to the committee boat. Buoys remain in place.)

"A word about the method used to establish the speed coefficients, or ratings, for the boats in the Friendship Sloop Regattas. The basic rating rule is that of the Storm Trysail Club for 1956 but, because all the boats are very similar, certain simplifications have been possible. The owners themselves can measure their boats, with the Society handicapper needing only to make some simple calculations to find the ratings.

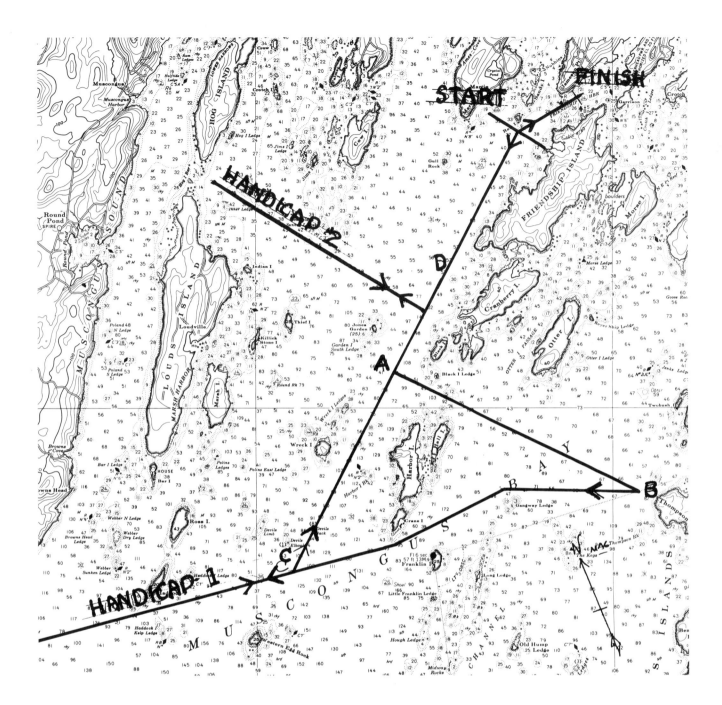

Friendship Sloop racing waters. A course of 12 miles might be from the starting line to buoy A, then to buoy B, and then to buoy C. From buoy C each Sloop must run down Handicap Alley 1 until she finds her own buoy. She must pick it up and return to round buoy C again and then continue to the finish line. Handicap Alley 2 could be used alternatively.

Bill Thon

A Friendship Sloop's handicap buoy.

"I have also added some refinements which I believe contribute toward greater fairness in handicapping for the Friendship Sloop Races. Among these are: credits for fixed interior accommodations; credit for cotton sails over Dacron; penalty for sails with battens; and, for the Original Sloops, a credit for age in the form of an increase in the allowed seconds per mile.

"In order to close up the competition still further, an effort is made to compensate for the indefinable characteristics which make one boat faster than its apparently identical sister, and to equalize the varying abilities and experience of the skippers. Penalties in the form of percentage increases in ratings are applied to boats which have placed in previous regattas. The penalty for a given boat builds up as it wins any

of the first three places in its class, and is reduced slightly for each race in which it competes but does not place. Over a period of time this penalty system not only allows the less experienced skippers a crack at the silverware, but also tends to place a premium on improvement rather than on absolute performance.

"In closing, I would like to say that I greatly enjoy working with the owners and officials of the Friendship Sloop Society, and am glad to contribute what time and knowledge I can to such a worthwhile venture."

Cy Hamlin

BUOYS AND ANCHORS

The picking up of the toggle buoy has created some harrowing moments. In the 1968 races, one of the toggle buoys came aboard and as the Sloop came about, the buoy skipped and bounded across the deck and splashed overboard on the opposite side, necessitating a rerun of the whole procedure.

The positions in which the buoys are set for handicapping is precise. In the first years of the Regatta, it was done by the Coast Guard, but in recent races, our perennial Race Committee Chairman, Bill Danforth, using the radar aboard his 36-foot *White Falcon*, has set them with pinpoint accuracy.

The preparation of the buoys for the Regatta is almost a story in itself, and while it takes several days to get them all ready and set, it really is a year 'round job. Each year as the last gun is fired and the smoke clears away, and all the confusion, and all the fun are over for another year, and as the first Sloop heads home, a Friendship lobsterman heads down the bay to pick up the marker buoys and the handicap buoys. Several hours later when he heaves into sight, he is a sight to behold, with over 30 flags waving in the breeze as he makes his way to Al Roberts' wharf.

Every anchor, every buoy, every flag, and every line worth salvaging is dumped out on the float, hauled up onto the wharf, loaded into Al's truck, and then passed up into the loft of a "fishhouse" for safe keeping until the next year. During the winter when things are quiet, a few more buoys are made, old "pot warp" is saved for new lines, gallon paint cans are hoarded for making anchors, and before you know it, summer is upon us and everything must be made ready again. So—down come the buoys, flags, lines, and anchors, and a check is made to see what is damaged or missing, and repairs are made and replacements furnished. The gallon paint cans are filled with cement to serve as anchors, lines are checked for rot, buoys are repaired, flags replaced or repainted and everything is set aside to be handy when the proper time comes. When the day before the races finally arrives, the anchor lines are carefully measured out and bent on to the trawl buoys and their anchors, and are lined up numerically on Al's float where the *White Falcon* is tied up. Bill Danforth and his retinue of helpers load them aboard and cast off to head down the bay and set them in their proper places. The small lobster buoys bearing the same number as the large trawl buoys are not attached until very early the next morning. Bill checks all the buoys each day to make sure none has drifted out of place or been cut off during the night.

Friendship Sloops weren't developed with racing in mind, but they're hardly slow boats, and it's a safe guess that the old time lobstermen themselves, never ones to turn down a chance for a "brush" with a rival Sloop, would get a big kick out of today's Friendship Sloop Regattas.

AL ROBERTS

IX

CRUISING FRIENDSHIP-WAY

by ROGER F. DUNCAN

As *Eastward* slipped quietly into Round Pond on the last of the afternoon southwester, I saw George Bondholder's sharp-bowed ocean racing yawl at anchor, her chrome winches and varnished rails ablaze in the low sun. We took in topsails and jibs and anchored at a respectful distance. I was still lowering the mainsail when George came alongside in his plastic dinghy propelled by a little outboard about big enough to mix a drink with. As we furled sails, he roamed around inspecting our real belaying pins, massive standing rigging and heavy blocks. With the vessel snugged down, we settled comfortably in the cockpit, offering a brief libation to whatever gods had been gracious enough to accord us this lovely evening.

"So this is a Friendship Sloop!" observed George. "Quite an antique! Does this old-time gear really work?"

"Well, we came around from Boothbay today and it worked all right."

"We came from York—under spinnaker all the way. How do you ever keep the mast in her with dead-eyes instead of turnbuckles? I notice your rigging is pretty slack."

"It *is* a little more trouble than turnbuckles. We set up the rigging as tight as we can with a tackle. Some people just hook the throat halyard onto the lanyard to pull it tight. Then we sail her a bit. When there gets to be a lot of slack in the lee rigging, we take up half of it, tack, and snug up the other side. Then we have just enough slack to let her work easy."

"Work easy!" said George. "You can't tune a boat that way. She ought to be real tight. We are going to bar rigging instead of wire next year. The mast, hull and rigging should form a rigid truss on which to set the sail."

"Not on this boat. Our mast is a solid spruce tree, and can stand a good deal of sideways strain. If we let her take a little strain sideways, she won't have to bear such an almighty downward thrust. The resilience of the lanyards, the wire, and the mast itself give her a little life."

Just as the sun set behind the Brown Church on the hill, George's alert captain, neat in khaki, stepped to the flag halyards, lowered the burgee and raised a plain blue pennant in its place. He took in the ensign and switched on the masthead light. Through the cabin ports shone the bright glare of an electric bulb and through the skylight the bleat of a radio oozed. I was impressed, but not enough to do much about it. We never take the Friendship burgee down; it keeps the gulls off. We have no ensign. I compromised by lighting our riding light and hanging it on the forestay with a bit of marline.

By this time the little Shipmate stove was

" 'So this is a Friendship Sloop!' observed George. 'Quite an antique! Does this old-time gear really work?' "

doing its work, sending an almost invisible column of sweet wood smoke aloft in the twilight. George was easily persuaded to stay for supper in the snug cabin lit by the soft light of gimballed lamps.

As the evening wore on, he became more and more interested in the simple efficiencies of our primitive rig, so we took the hint and invited him to cruise with us for a day or two while his son and the paid skipper took *Salatia* on to Camden.

The next morning his son churned him alongside in the outboard as we were recovering from our morning dive overboard.

"Good heavens, have you been overboard?" George cried, "On purpose?"

"Don't you ever go in?" I asked the boy.

"Not without a fight," he answered as he pushed off.

We lingered over the coffee for it was still stark calm, and with the ebb tide running, there was little prospect of wind for several hours. *Salatia* spat a quid of smoke and water from her stern; the skipper took the shiny wheel while the boy took the anchor rope to an electric winch on the foredeck.

"They have to stop in Port Clyde for diesel oil because there isn't water enough at the float here with the tide going," said George. "They'll make Camden tonight all right. Don't you think we better start along? We have a fair tide down the Sound and could knock off ten miles or so under power before the wind comes in."

"If you are going cruising with us, George, you go our way," said Mary. "We are not really sure that there is an engine under the hatch anyway. Let's go ashore and see if we can get some more of that good cheese up at the store."

With the washing-up done, we rowed ashore in the peapod and walked up a path through a hayfield. Sparrows flipped out of the grass and Mary stopped to pick a late wild strawberry.

At the store we found a great wheel of Wisconsin cheese, of which we bought a solid chunk and then discovered that the storekeeper had invented a mackerel rig that was a certified fish-killer. No mackerel swam in the Gulf of Maine

"George seemed much interested in the slack in the head stays . . . "

who could resist that lure. It had only yesterday come in several times with a fish on each of its five hooks. If it caught no fish, no fish were there. Impressed, we bought two and headed back for the shore as the faded flag over the post office showed the beginnings of a southerly air.

With George on the peak halyard, we set the mainsail. He was impressed with the way the set of the gaff could change the draft of the sail. Because the breeze was light, we left the sail a little full. Out of a tangle of gear the topsail went aloft and was sheeted home, looking very simple once it was up. George hauled the anchor by main strength and ignorance. As the sloop paid off, Mary set staysail, jib, and jib topsail. The peapod turned and followed us by the can at the entrance and we hauled on the wind.

George at the main sheet snugged it down hard, almost amidships, and I headed about 45 degrees to the wind to beat down the Sound. *Eastward,* outraged at the treatment, stopped.

"I knew a Friendship was slow to windward, but I had no idea she was this slow. Why the bubbles are scarcely going by at all. Does she need a gale of wind to move her?"

I slacked the main sheet until the boom was over the quarter, fell off nearly a point (about 11 degrees), while Mary eased headsail sheets. Slowly *Eastward* gathered way and was soon making a little bubble under her bow. She slipped easily along at nearly four knots in the light air, leaving a flat wake astern.

"You can't pinch her, George. She won't stand it. You have to ease your main sheet and give her a mouth full, but then she'll go all right. Pinch her up to the wind and she'll die on you."

We approached the lobster traps on the Loud's Island shore. There are boulders scattered with a generous hand all along here, so Mary let go jib and jib topsail sheets to port, I rolled the wheel over and stepped to the starboard side to trim the headsails on the new tack as she came round. I reached behind me to straighten the wheel and felt George's hand on the spokes.

63

"I thought I better get hold of it; you had both hands busy."

"She's all right. You don't have to steer her every minute; but since you have her, take her along a bit."

George assumed an alert air, looked under the mainsail at the luff of the staysail, turned the wheel a bit and then slowly kept turning it to port. Suddenly he reversed it as *Eastward* rushed up into the wind all a-luff, then bore off again. But he soon got the feel of her, and found it necessary to give her only a spoke now and then. She responded much more deliberately than his larger yawl, because of her weight, her deep forefoot, and her long straight keel. Running before a sea, while a challenge to a helmsman in any boat, is much easier in a Friendship sloop because the long keel holds her on a straight course.

As we tacked off Brown's Head, Mary rigged a mackerel line and paid it out astern. We could fetch easily now between Ross and Haddock Islands so started sheets. George was not sure about fishing under way, but he didn't say anything. It was part of our routine to try the fish if the breeze fell light. We have even been known to anchor in light weather off Pemaquid Point, Bantam Rock, or Isle au Haut and jig up a codfish.

We passed south of Webber's Dry Ledge where the seals were lying on the rockweed. It occurred to us that a seal leads a sybaritic life in Maine in the summer. Except for an occasional shark, he has no enemies. There is plenty to eat. He spends the day lying in the sun or playing in the surf, his only embarrassment the passing excursion-boat whose public address system points him out to tourists with binoculars and cameras. Yet I never saw a seal blush.

I noticed Mary's line tighten and a taut expression on her face as she hauled in steadily, hand over hand. Standing on the house, I could see the line sweep across the wake and back and could make out two white streaks as the mackerel fought. I slacked the main sheet and fetched the bucket. *Eastward* slowed, and in a splash of salt water not two, but three, fat mackerel were drumming on the after deck.

We picked our way through the ledges, by the Devil's Elbow, Franklin Island, and Gangway Ledge as the breeze increased. We took in the jib topsail after a bit because the topmast was showing the strain and setting up backstays was a nuisance. She went pretty close to hull speed anyway.

As we approached the narrow passage between Thompson and Barter Islands going nearly seven knots under quite a press of sail, George looked a little worried. He held the chart, studying the narrow slot of deep water between the half-tide rocks of Thompson Island and the shoal on the Barter Island side.

"There aren't any buoys in here. How do you know where the end of the ledge is off Thompson Island?" Mary answered that one:

"We know because we hit it once."

"What happened?"

"Oh nothing much. We hit her quite a rap but she bounced over and no harm done. An iron shoe and a long heavy oak keel can take quite a bump."

"How about the Barter Island side. Did you hit that too?"

"No, but you follow just outside the line of lobster traps until you get nearly to the point and then head for Gig Rock bell. You will probably see the loom of a white ledge over to port because it is about low water." We slipped through and bore off for the passage off Marshall Point.

We had a grand sail by Port Clyde. George seemed much interested in the slack in the head stays and the absence of a permanent backstay or any other means of holding the mast from falling over the bow. The shrouds were set far enough aft to help some, but mostly we relied on the strength of the spar itself. It bent, but it seemed to stay there.

"Within fifteen minutes the fog shut down."

"*Eastward* thundered under her lee bow . . ."

Off the Brothers the wind began to fade, and by the time we got to Mosquito Bell it had fallen quite light. When Mary went out on the bowsprit to take the stops off the jib topsail, George looked a little apprehensive. He glanced at the life ring to be sure it was clear just in case, but the bowsprit shrouds, forestay, bobstay, and jibstay afforded secure support, and no emergency developed.

We headed ENE for Whitehead and had a lunch, the cheese proving a great success.

The breeze was well out to the south now and felt colder. The sky had hazed up a good deal and Two-Bush was only dimly visible. While we were cleaning up, the long blast of the horn sounded and soon Whitehead joined it. Within fifteen minutes the fog shut down.

We hung up a reflector in the rigging and kept on. We had no radar, we had no fathometer, we had no patent log, we started no engine. With a glance overside I estimated our speed at four knots. The flood tide would set us up into the Muscle Ridge Channel somewhere. We could just hear the deep bell off Tenant's Harbor. We lost the horn on Whitehead. For some

strange reason it is inaudible to the southwest within two miles, although you can hear it 10 miles away in Friendship on a quiet day.

Under sail in the fog, sounds became of great significance. The wash of the bow wave, the squeaking of gaff jaws, even the rhythmic blasts of distant horn and bell became part of the background against which the howl of an approaching sardiner's high-speed diesel, or the distant growl of a yacht engine were important. Someone was hauling lobster traps along the Crow Island shore, his engine racing and idling by spells. A pot buoy appeared on the lee bow, seemed to be hurrying on some business of its own as it passed close ahead, and disappeared on the weather quarter.

Suddenly we heard the blast of Whitehead's horn, and the jangle of the Southeast Breaker bell. The bell swept by invisible to starboard. The horn drew closer, then higher off the water, and we were tossed by the backwash off the cliff. A minute later and we sailed out of the curtain of fog into the bright sun and could see all the way to Ash Island and Otter Island, but a bank of fog lay over Penobscot Bay.

65

Before the gentle air we sailed up the channel with a fair tide, again with fish line over the stern. Out of the fog burst the sardiner we had heard, heavily loaded and bound for Southwest Harbor, her radar receiver whirling—a business-like vessel. From ahead came a tall sloop under power, her mainsail under a blue sail cover and a jib bagged at the foot of the forestay. One man stood at the tiller, impassive before the compass, and waved politely. A lobster boat roared out of Spruce Head, on wings of spray, her radio going full blast and a pot buoy at a cocky angle on the house roof. The fisherman slowed around our stern, read our name, and waved enthusiastically.

It was getting on into the afternoon. George thought we could make Camden all right.

"We have four or five hours of daylight, a good enough breeze and a fair tide. There is a bell outside Camden on the Graves and a fog signal on Curtis Island. We can always run the engine if we have to, and with a good compass, the fog is no problem." I was opposed.

"The wind will die in another couple of hours, it is thick as mud outside and no fun. Camden will be socked in tight so you can't see the hills. Besides, those great tankers going up to Searsport scare me. Let's hang up in Dix Island. I haven't been ashore there for a long time.

Perhaps remembering that he came cruising with us to see how we did it, George welcomed the decision. We worked our way into the harbor among the ledges, the topsail full when the heavier mainsail hung slack; we disturbed some comfortable seals, started an osprey, and slipped easily into the anchorage. Jib and top-sail came down on the run, then staysail, mainsail, and anchor.

Presently we rowed ashore and found a camp with dish towels on the line but no one home. We climbed a pile of old grout, looked into the quarry, bushwhacked through thick spruce woods broken with glades of grass, clumps of juniper, and bare ledge. Sun-warmed raspberries delayed us. A white-throat sang piercingly in the warmth of spruce and sweet fern. At length we came out on the shore again to see the fog shutting in over the outer islands, feel the chill southerly wind and smell the sharp saltwater smell again. We followed around the shore back to our peapod, noticing evidence of what had once been a very profitable granite quarry. We found a pot buoy in a pile of rotting rockweed, we skipped some flat stones across the water, startled sandpipers and turnstones, and watched an osprey wheel screaming over a school. We stopped, hoping to see him dive; but after hovering on beating wings, he wheeled off down wind in a long glide.

At the anchorage we found a lobster boat and a family just come ashore. The brown barefoot children streaked for the camp and the radio. Elbridge and his wife June introduced themselves, and as they gathered bundles from the dory told us they came down from Rockland during the summers for the lobstering and to tend the weir. They had just been "up town" to sell their lobsters, stock up at the grocery store and visit with their neighbors. They had come in just ahead of the fog.

It had shut down thick, sifting through the trees and lying gray and heavy on the calm water. George had goose bumps on his bare legs below the Breton-red shorts. Our cabin was dank and dark, but the lamps and stove soon had it snug.

After a supper in which the mackerel figured prominently I was on deck sloshing the dishpan over the side when I heard the clunk of oars and out of the fog rowed Elbridge.

Mary poured coffee with a touch of red rum to keep out the cold and Elbridge told us of lobstering among the ledges in January when the sea was streaked with vapor and you had to keep your woolen mittens wet so as not to freeze your hands. He told us of the loss of the Vinalhaven ferry in a northwest gale that

"Late in the afternoon, we sailed up Camden Harbor . . ."

stove in a forehatch, filled her forward hold so she wouldn't steer, and soon sank her. The crew made it to Leadbetter's Island on a raft whence they were rescued. He told of taking $15,000 worth of herring out of the weir on one tide and of never seeing a fin all the next summer. He sang us a song of The War of 1812 which his father and grandfather used to sing, beginning

"Ye Parliaments of England,
        Ye Lords and Commons too,
Consider well what you're about
        and what you're going to do.
You're going to fight with Yankees,
        I'm sure you'll rue the day,
You've roused the sons of Liberty
        in North America-y."

And went on to deal accurately with every American naval victory in the war. We wound up the evening talking about Rockland schools and his ambitions for his boys.

After he left, we turned in and fell asleep to the counterpoint of the horns on Whitehead and Two Bush and the wash of the tide on the ledges.

Some time during the night I wakened to a roll of thunder, a rush of wind and rain, and the squeak of the anchor rode on the bitt. I looked out the hatch and in the beam of the big flashlight could make out the point of the island through the slanting rain. The anchor held, the squall passed, and through the hatch I saw a star.

Morning was crystal. The Camden hills, the nearby spruces, the islands to seaward, the low line of Vinalhaven seemed carved in delicate dark wood. We got under way early, waved to Elbridge hauling traps under High Island, and stood to the eastward across Penobscot Bay. The northerly breeze was fresh, but we carried

Robert Thing

topsail, staysail, and jib. *Eastward* thundered under her lee bow, left a broad white wake astern, and only occasionally tossed us a capful of spray over her shoulder. George stood to the wheel, easing her a bit in the puffs to claw to windward, and felt the drumming, exhilarating power of 700 square feet of canvas driving nine tons of boat at seven knots.

We had a grand sail across the Bay, tacked, and started back. But the wind faded between Owl's Head and Vinalhaven although yellow smoke from the cement factory still flowed in a long dirty streak towards us. The water grew silky, the sun grew hot, the mainsheet slacked and banged its block on the traveller, and we ghosted gently westward.

George began to look at the engine hatch, but we pretended not to notice. Mary got a mackerel line over the side. I unrove the weather jib sheet and took a twist out of it. We watched the ferry cross toward North Haven and heard the gong buoy ring as her wake rocked it. Far up the Bay a red and white spinnaker bloomed where the northerly still blew. The Camden Hills stood behind the shore.

We drifted on, slatting occasionally, caught no mackerel, and were at length becalmed—at considerable length becalmed—and warmly so.

Presently, down the Bay appeared a line of fresher blue. Two Bush and Hurricane Island began to look a little dusty. The burgee lifted and flopped to the north, the main boom squeaked over, we felt a cool breath of sea air and the southerly had struck in.

Late in the afternoon, we sailed up Camden Harbor and took a mooring near *Salatia*, gleaming, trim and taut. We furled up and snugged down. George seemed in no hurry to leave so we sat in the cockpit together and watched one of the cruise schooners sail up the harbor, round to, drop sails and push up to her wharf with her yawl-boat. There seemed to be a good deal to be said for doing things the old way.

X

ENDURING FRIENDSHIPS

By James S. Rockefeller, Jr.

On a starlit evening, back in a time we are still living, the mountains of Tahiti loomed dark and inviting behind the breaking reef and Papeete Harbor. When the range lights came in line, the old Friendship eased through the pass onto the placid surface of the lagoon and was tied to a mooring dolphin until officialdom should sanctify her arrival the following morning.

We settled in the cockpit, two salt-encrusted youths, and sniffed the zephyr wafting down from the hills so scented with the perfume of Tiara Tahiti as to make one choke. Along the waterfront, backlighted by the quayside street, a row of trading schooners lay silhouetted against the sea wall, while from deep in the town came the pulse of music—that joy-loving heartbeat of Polynesia. To further sugar that capsule in time, down the quay sauntered two black-tressed beauties strumming guitars. They broke their stroll directly landward of our boat and offered a greeting.

"Wouldn't that gag a goat!" my shipmate exploded. "All that water we've put under us and here we rot! Look at all that livin' going down the drain!"

It was amusing. Here we were, quivering observers, impotent but to smell, watch, listen, and clutch our thoughts. Chuckling, I flopped on my back and gazed up at the stars trying to blot out the sight of those South Sea sirens in their idyllic frame. With infinite concentration, I worked my thoughts out the pass to windward, out amidst the rough and tumble of the trades and the soaring birds, back along the track we'd come in an effort to beguile the moment.

A lot of water had slid along the keel, that was true. A lot of water and a lot of living—a lot of a lot of things. It involved two pump leathers, drums of elbow grease, and a dream come true. There was a keg of boat nails, cuprinol, anxiety, and joy. My toe explored the rough planks of the deck. A boat, a little ship, was more than just a thing of wood and canvas. A boat was like life, in that you got out of it what you put in. A year I had spent rebuilding this old girl, with Tahiti just a far-off dream. I knew how tired she was beneath the paint. How well I knew her punky frames, her pine planking so waterlogged it would barely hold paint, her weeping butts spewing cotton. I thought no less of her. We were old, old friends, the two of us, and we had made the dream come true.

To build and sail a boat—men have marched and nations fallen rallying to calls of lesser weight and sound. Since the animals went two

"A year I had spent rebuilding this old girl, with Tahiti just a far-off dream." (The *Mandalay* in the South Pacific.)

Courtesy, James S. Rockefeller, Jr.

by two and Moses floated safe within the reeded basket, man has pounded, lashed, and stuck the stuff together to shape floating cockleshells in which to freight his lust and longing, achieve ambitions high and low, or save his skin. To build or buy a boat and sail away; surely a goodly portion of the human experience is cradled here.

That night aboard my Friendship in Papeete Harbor, I couldn't realize that today I would be in a boatshop of my own, eyeing two Friendships under construction. Life is an evolutionary process. Our yesterdays lead us to the present, and continuity helps make a life complete and purposeful.

With a certain wonder I walk over to examine the first of these new Sloops in the making. She is planked with native cedar on our native oak. The fastenings are bronze, the chainplates bronze, the keel a ton of lead. Under the teak decking of the cockpit is tucked a two-cylinder diesel of European make. The cabin is all white with mahogany trim, and there are four berths although the boat is only 25 feet long. On the aft bulkhead is an electrical panel with a gang

of switches, while the toilet has an elaborate attachment to treat sewage according to the latest regulations. Looking out the mahogony hatch I see the mahogony wheel on the bronze steering mechanism.

Patting the mahogany cap rail, I go over to the other Sloop and run my hand over the hull. She is absolutely smooth—no seams, imperfections, not even a bung shows. I tap this phenomenon of the boatbuilder's art and am rewarded by a drumlike thrum. On deck and below she looks like the other Sloop, but under the cabin sole I know the water and fuel tanks are an integral part of the fiberglass hull. There are no shelf, clamp, or frames, so there is slightly more room below.

On the long bench are the blocks. They are beautiful things with lignumvitae cheeks and bronze sheaves, quite unlike the crude commercial ones on my old boat. Alongside these lie the bronze main gooseneck and gaff saddle gleaming like new gold.

The shop is closed for the day. Winter twilight is on the way, and my thoughts float somewhere between Tahiti and this high hill over-

70

Jarvis Newman

"To build or buy a boat and sail away; surely a goodly portion of the human experience is cradled here." (The *Salatia*.)

Carlton Simmons

"Is it the saucy sheer, the tumblehome around the transom, the trailboards capped by the rugged bowsprit with its dangling gaskets to secure the jib?"

looking Penobscot Bay. Leaning against the bench my eyes wander over the two Sloops, waiting in their stocks.

Little jewels they are, a far cry from my old girl who rolled me down the Pacific trades. They are better boats by far, foot for foot, built for pleasure, and to last. Yet something precious has been lost; something just as precious gained. My old Friendship was of a different time, a different place, and now that time is done. I envision no sweat and blood, no rotten gear, frozen hands or aching muscles before me here. I do not see those rust streaks that must have worried grizzled heads on those stormy winter days when the bread still had to be wrested from the sea. I see no rotten frames, no weeping butts, no roofing paper on

the fore deck to keep out the leaks, no big seam along the turn of the bilge to speak of old age, sloppy construction, poverty and neglect.

The bad has gone, the age has gone, but the good, the romance, the continuity remains. These two Sloops have a certain something that warms the heart and makes one ponder. Is it the saucy sheer, the tumblehome around the transom, the trailboards capped by the rugged bowsprit with its dangling gaskets to secure the jib? Is it the low profile of the house and the gracefully rounded cockpit, the unbroken symmetry of the backbone? No one thing, perhaps, rather a blending of the whole. There is an aura of honesty; no gimmicks and the proportions are right. Chrome and glass and gadgetry are strangers here. These Sloops "look up to

71

"The Sloops will sail . . . " (The *Sazerac,* opposite page.)

"New boats are being built . . . " (Bill Thon christening his *Echo.*)

their work," ready for a thrash against a blustery Nor'wester, or just as eager to slide along under the push of a gentle Southerly. A glimmer of their working heritage remains, and we are carried back to a simpler time when dreams came true and wind and tide held fair, or so we like to tell ourselves.

The stuff of dreams, this is what boats are all about. A bit of magic is a basic need in life, get it where you will. Take the owners of these two Sloops: they chose, instead of one of the thousands of designs, or one of the myriad stock boats readily available, a Friendship Sloop to satisfy their need. They decided on a boat from out of the past; they are willing to sacrifice accommodation and headroom below, willing to reef and hand a large mainsail with a longer boom, in order to be a part of the past, to have a sense of belonging to something bigger than the boat, herself.

This same feeling drew me to my old boat the first time I saw her lying in a Southern port, nearly derelict, with paint peeling and rigging slack. She was rigged a ketch, one of the few ever built, and someone had put a raised deck and bulwarks on her. Yet the Friendship in her still stood out, that certain something which smacked of bold shores, spruce trees, and a bubbling wake.

Friendships are more than just a pleasure to the eye. They take our minds and spin them down a hundred different paths. They stand for white lighthouses on a rocky shore, lobster traps piled on a fish house wharf, a flock of sheep browsing on a treeless islet, the moon rising behind Isle Au Haut, the fog creeping up the Narrows on a Southeast wind, or the moan of a buoy heaving seaward in the swells. They stand for fishermen tugging at the twine, and gimbaled lamps glowing in a land-locked cove.

What is the future for these very special boats? There is a Society now with members from all over. New boats are being built, trailboards fitted, billetheads carved. No longer is Wilbur Morse carved along the grape leaf

scroll, but other men have taken his place, each with his own distinctive touch.

Dedicated people give their time and energy to keep the Sloops alive and growing in number. For the Sloops are more than lovely character boats with a past. They have become a symbol of more than just an age. They stand for good fellowship in the rounded cockpit amidst clean air and good water. They stand for a job well done, a day well lived, and Maine. They have come to mean a yearly occasion when character boats and the people who love them gather in a coastal town to shape and preserve a time and place where decency, fun, and humor serve as a breakwater against the grinding of our modern world.

The boats no doubt in time will change. Fewer wooden ones will slide down the ways, for money must have its say. Shape, however, is more important than material if the workmanship is good and the material sound. Perhaps even the shape will alter, for this is a product of man's mind, and time and new horizons push and shove unmercifully.

But the symbol will remain, this golden thread we can follow through the labyrinth of the future. The Sloops will sail with their creaking gaffs as long as this symbol doesn't tarnish and die, even though shape and time and people come and go. It is people who build and sail the Sloops. It is people who gather once a year in Friendship to renew and strengthen the symbol. It is people who set the course and man the wheel.

There is an old Norse legend about a little bird who once a year on his annual migration perches atop a rock way up near the Arctic Circle. This rock is a mile high and a mile wide and a mile long. In the middle of this colossus the little bird alights and sharpens his bill. Let us hope that people will flock to Friendship once a year to see the sailing of the Sloops for as long as it takes that little bird, sharpening his bill once a year, to crack that giant rock asunder.

XI

A CATALOG OF FRIENDSHIPS

by Al Roberts

At the time of this writing there are ninety-seven Sloops registered in the Friendship Sloop Society. They are presented here according to their Society numbers, which are assigned chronologically as owners join the Society. At the end of this section there is a list of the Sloops alphabetically by name, as a cross-reference.

Where no photograph of a given Sloop appears, it is because neither our local photographers nor the owner could provide one.

As indicated in Chapter VIII, the criteria for the Class designations A, B, C, and D are as follows:

Class A—Sloops built prior to 1921

Class B—Sloops built since 1921 following strictly the lines of the originals

Class C—replica Sloops that deviate slightly from the original lines

Class D—Sloops with other than wooden hull construction.

The abbreviations used for the dimensions are LOA for length-over-all, LWL for length on the water line, B for beam, and D for draft.

As a matter of interest concerning racing participation, twenty-five individual races have been scheduled since and including the first race in 1961; six of these have had to be cancelled due to either lack of wind or no lack of fog, so that nineteen races have been sailed up through and including the 1969 Regatta.

1

VOYAGER
Class A
John Kippin, Ipswich, Massachusetts
built by Charles Morse, 1902
LOA—29′ 6″ LWL—24′ B—9′ 6″ D—4′ 10″
9 races; 1 first, 1 second, 1 third

This is the Sloop that started it all. She sailed so well in a Boston Power Squadron Race that her owner, then Bernard MacKenzie, conceived the idea of a Homecoming Race for Friendship Sloops in Friendship. Beside being founder of the Friendship Sloop Society, Bernard MacKenzie is a past president and honorary lifetime president.

Note *Voyager's* raised roof for full headroom.

Carlton Simmons

2

DICTATOR
Class A
Peter Chesney, Deer Isle, Maine
built by Robert McLain, 1904
LOA—31′ 6″ B—11′ 6″ D—5′ 6″

FINETTE
Class A
Frank Smith, Wethersfield, Connecticut
built by Wilbur A. Morse, 1915
LOA—47′ LWL—36′ 1″ B—11′ 7″ D—6′ 3″

Golden Eagle's skipper sailed her from Marblehead to Friendship for four regattas. Some of these trips he made alone, as in 1964 when he was fogged in at Boothbay, but still arrived in time for the Saturday race.

Here, he has plenty of able-bodied help aboard.

GOLDEN EAGLE
Class A
William Haskell, Marblehead, Massachusetts
built by A. F. Morse, 1910
LOA—26′ 10″ LWL—24′ B—8′ 10″ D—4′ 6″
7 races; 2 seconds, 2 thirds

Carlton Simmons

5

CONTENT
Class B
Robert Edwards, Montclair, New Jersey
built by Stuart M. Ford, 1961
LOA—25′ LWL—21′ B—8′ 7″ D—4′ 3″
15 races; 1 third

Many of us remember seeing the *Content's* 76-year-old owner-builder sitting in a boatswains chair at 6:30 A.M. doing some rigging work at the top of his mast. A broken hip later forced him to sell his beloved Sloop. He said, "I want her to go to someone who will love her." Stu found that someone in the family of Robert Edwards. Just wait until the Army lets Peter free, and he and his father will show what the *Content* can do.

As she beats out of the harbor, the crew stows the anchor on deck. Note her roller-furling jib.

Carlton Simmons

Eastward is a legend along the Maine Coast where she cruises with charter parties and helps her author-skipper seek out information for his book, *Cruising Guide to the New England Coast*. She is also a legend in the Society, winning many races and thereby increasing her handicap to the point where Handicap Alley is not long enough. Roger may have to row ashore and dig a hod of clams as part of his handicap, it is rumored. Roger was our third president. Murray Peterson designed *Eastward*.

See how she slips along in the light air, with Roger making sure his jib topsail is doing its work. On second thought, if it's light on race day, maybe he'd better dig two hods.

EASTWARD 6
Class B
Roger and Mary Duncan, Newagen, Maine, and
  West Concord, Massachusetts
built by James Chadwick, 1956
LOA—32′ 1″ LWL—27′ B—10′ 6″ D—5′ 4″
18 races; 8 firsts, 3 seconds, 2 thirds

7

TANNIS II
Class B
John D. Cronin, Sturbridge, Massachusetts
built by W. S. Carter, 1937
LOA—38′ LWL—32′ B—12′ D—6′
3 races

The *Tannis II* has changed hands from Douglas Randall to Frank Niering, and now to her present owner, John Cronin. She really is a family boat, having raced in the 1969 Regatta with John and Mary and all six Cronin children aboard. The youngest gave orders from a playpen set up in the cockpit.

This Sloop also has her jib set flying on a luff wire that can be twisted by rotating the roller drum visible at the bowsprit end by means of a hauling line that leads from the drum in on deck. This results in rolling the jib up on its luff wire like a window shade, a handy method of furling that can be accomplished in just a few seconds.

Carlton Simmons

BANSHEE
Class A
Benjamin Waterworth, New Bedford,
    Massachusetts
built by Morse
LOA—30′ LWL—25′ B—9′ 6″ D—4′ 6″

8

9

The *Amity* is one of the spectators' favorite
Sloops, but she has not been able to make the
last few Regattas. Now that her owner is retired
from the Washington Post and his Ambassador-
ship to the United Nations, we hope she'll be
back.

Note her bell, tiller, and husky main sheet
blocks.

AMITY
Class A
James Russell Wiggins, Brooklin, Maine
built by Wilbur A. Morse, 1900
LOA—30′ B—12′ D—5′
4 races; 3 firsts, 1 second

MARY ANNE
Class B

10

Doctor Joe Griffin, Damariscotta, Maine
built by Lash Brothers, 1958
LOA—30′ LWL—25′ B—9′ 6″ D—4′ 9″
6 races; 2 seconds, 1 third

John Dallett, *Mary Anne's* former owner, cut down her mast and boom from his previous boat, a schooner. Doctor Griffin, her new owner, sailed her in the 1969 races.

Her staysail is set flying, so that when it is lowered, there is no forestay in the way of the jib. Note the netting under her bowsprit.

Carlton Simmons

The *Old Friendly* sailed in the first Regatta as *L'Aigle D'Or*. Since then she has been sold a couple of times, but we are earnestly hoping that her present owner can get enough time away from the School of Education at the University of Massachusetts to bring her back to Friendship.

See how she ghosts along on one of those sunny-hazy days.

OLD FRIENDLY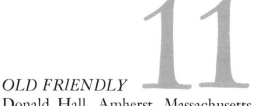
Donald Hall, Amherst, Massachusetts
built by Warren Prescott Gannet, 1938
LOA—24′ LWL—20′ B—7′ D—3′ 6″
1 race

FRIENDSHIP
Robert Cavanaugh, Compton, Rhode Island
built by Wilbur A. Morse, 1902
LOA—29′ 6″ LWL—25′ 3″ B—9′ 9″ D—4′ 6″

13

EASTING
Class B
James R. Pierpont, Milford, Connecticut
built by C. A. Morse, 1920
LOA—29′ 8″ LWL—23′ B—9′ 6″ D—5′ 4″

Reports have it that James Pierpont has had a long rebuilding struggle, but plans to bring the *Easting* to Friendship for a Regatta.

14

VIGOR
Class B
Robert K. Emerson, Hancock Point, Maine
built by Morse Boat Yard, 1946
LOA—30′ LWL—26′ B—9′ 8″ D—4′ 6″
19 races

The former *Sadie M*, now the *Vigor*, has been to Friendship for every race. In 1967, Harry Prindle changed her spoon bow to the traditional clipper bow. Harry and his Maine Maritime School crew became an integral part of the Society, and Robert Emerson is carrying on the tradition.

Who wouldn't trade places with the lad on the bowsprit?

Carlton Simmons

You can always count on Ted Brown and his son Timmy to be in the thick of the fight, racing, or helping any way they can, from rescuing Sloops dragging anchor, to measuring buoy mooring lines, to correcting compasses, to almost anything. Timmy even deserts ship to help on the *White Falcon*, the Race Committee boat. (He is one of the boys in the loud pants.)

Photographers say the *Vida Mia* is always posing between their lenses and pretty clouds.

Irving Nevells

15

VIDA MIA
Class C
Frederick S. Brown, Kittery, Maine
built by E. L. Stevens, 1942
LOA—30′ LWL—24′ 6″ B—10′ D—4′ 9″
19 races; 2 seconds, 6 thirds

RETRIEVER 16

Class B
John Rice, Scituate, Massachusetts
built by Warren Prescott Gannet, 1942
LOA—22′ 4″ LWL—19′ 3″ B—7′ 6″ D—3′ 6″
4 races; 1 third

John Rice really can sail that *Retriever*, but he had a hard time in Friendship with anchors. First he couldn't get the anchor to hold, and then he couldn't get it to break out. He finally got her aboard, though.

Note her loose-footed forestaysail and generous jib.

Carlton Simmons

Dick Swanson, *Jolly Buc's* former owner, was our second president. This Sloop really is a character boat. When she sailed into Friendship for her first Regatta, she had tan-barked sails and 18,000 ax heads in her hold for ballast. She sprang a leak straining in a heavy breeze during the 1962 Regatta and had to withdraw, but she came right back the next year and won the third race. Now that Dick has sold her to Bill Johnson, this queen of the fleet sails in southern waters.

Her topsail has just been lowered in the lee of the mainsail and is being smothered on deck.

JOLLY BUCCANEER
Class A
Bill Johnson, Miami, Florida
built by McLain, 1909
LOA—45′ LWL—40′ B—13′ D—7′ 6″
8 races; 1 first, 1 second, 1 third

17

Carlton Simmons

CHRISSY
Class A
Ernst Wiegleb, Pleasant Point, Maine
built by Charles Morse, 1912
LOA 29' 8" LWL—25' B—9' D—5'
18 races; 10 firsts, 3 seconds, 1 third

18

Named for Ernie Wiegleb's wife, *Chrissy* has been in every Regatta but the first. She didn't like New Jersey or New York waters, and protested by having a scuffle with a bridge in New York. She now graces the Pleasant Point, Maine, harbor, and with her crew of Ernie and his sons is a tough boat to beat.

She's in great shape for a boat nearly 60 years old.

Carlton Simmons

Bill Pendleton, who started the Society's Scholarship Fund, has another favorite of the spectators in *Blackjack*. She has raced every year, placed well, and can be readily identified by her black hull and varnished cabin. (Also by the hearty laughs from Bill and his crew, Sam Calderwood.)

Here, she chuckles along herself at the age of 69.

19

BLACKJACK
Class A
William Pendleton, Suffield, Connecticut, and
    Searsport, Maine
built by Wilbur A. Morse, 1900
LOA—33′
19 races; 2 firsts, 7 seconds, 5 thirds

Carlton Simmons

20

JOEANNA
Class A
Charles Newman, Gloucester, Massachusetts
built by Morse, 1910
LOA—30′ LWL—27′ B—11′ D—5′ 6″
6 races

When Bob Trays owned her, she was the *Wanderer*. We remember the year the *Wanderer* and *Retriever* both signed up to race, but neither appeared. We figured the *Retriever* was out after the *Wanderer*. Charles Newman brought the *Joeanna* into Friendship on Saturday of the 1969 races, but not in time to race. We hope he will be back.

Note the parrel beads instead of mast hoops.

Elmer Barde

The *Wilbur Morse* has stayed in Friendship where she was built. The Friendship Sloop Regatta would not seem the same without Wilfred Brann and his *Wilbur Morse*. He has raced every year.

Note the spare mast hoops kept just above the boom so a broken one could be replaced without unrigging the mast to slide the new hoop on.

WILBUR MORSE
Class B
C. Wilfred Brann, Gardiner, Maine
built by Carlton Simmons, 1947
LOA—30′ 2″ LWL—26′ B—9′ 6″ D—4′ 9″
19 races

21

Carlton Simmons

22

ELLIE T
Class B
John Thorpe, Woolwich, Maine
built by John Thorpe, 1961
LOA—25' 8" LWL—21' 8" B—8' 6" D—4' 6"
19 races; 2 seconds, 7 thirds

The *Ellie T* was built from the *Pemaquid* plans by the son of the man who owned the *Pemaquid*. She has sailed in every race. Her crewman, Paul Bryant, has in the years of racing graduated from deckhand, to part-time skipper, to son-in-law.

The skipper holds the sheet as a little puff off the land sends her foaming along.

Irving Nevells

The *Depression* is probably the oldest Friendship Sloop still sailing. She has raced in part of every Regatta but the first, and somehow manages to bring her Boston doctor home last every year. She was sold for $15.00 during the Depression, which accounts for her name.

She has a mighty pretty bow.

DEPRESSION **23**
Class A
Doctor Myron Hahn, Boston, Massachusetts, and Friendship, Maine
built 1899
LOA—32′ LWL—26′ 4″ B—9′ D—5′ 6″
8 races

Carlton Simmons

ANCIENT MARINER
Class A
Holt C. Vibber, Waterford, Connecticut
built by Wilbur A. Morse
LOA—26′ LWL—20′ 9″ B—8′ 6″ D—4′ 6″

24

She was once known as the *Tern*, but knowing she was built by Wilbur Morse, her owner decided that *Ancient Mariner* was a better name. She is being completely rebuilt.

SEA DUCK
Laurence Bershad, Marblehead, Massachusetts
built by Morse Boat Yard
LOA—36' B—12' D—6'

The *Sea Duck* is a ketch and races in Massachusetts. She has never come to Friendship for the races. She went to the aid of the *Eagle* the year the *Eagle* was dismasted in the Marblehead Race.

VIRGINIA M.
Class A
Jaxon Vibber, Waterford, Connecticut
built by Wilbur A. Morse, 1910
LOA—28' LWL—22' 10" B—8' 11" D—4' 6"

This old Sloop gradually slipped until she was about gone, but Jaxon Vibber has bought her and is going to fight off Father Time with a rebuilding job.

She is shown here with a single-head rig.

YANKEE TRADER
Class B
Eric W. Osborn, Bristol, Rhode Island
built by Bob McKean and Sid Carter, 1939
LOA—28' LWL—20' B—8' 4" D—4' 6"

The *Yankee Trader* will fly her owner's national flag—the British Ensign. Eric Osborn is all set to win a Regatta with her.

BOUNTY
Class B
Doctor Roy Gumpel, Rye, New York
built by Warren Prescott Gannet
LOA—22' 8" LWL—18' B—7' 6" D—3' 6"

We are still hoping Doctor Roy Gumpel will bring her from New York to Maine for a Regatta.

28

Loving care at the hands of N. Bradford Mack has kept this original alive. He races her in Florida waters where she makes a good account of herself.

Her sailmaker-owner uses a genoa jib to help her along, here in combination with a reefed mainsail. Her flush deck aft and high rail are unusual.

29

SUSAN
Class A
N. Bradford Mack, South Miami, Florida
built by Wilbur A. Morse, 1902
LOA—41' LWL—36' B—13' 6" D—5' 9"

30

KIDNAPPED
LOA—21′ LWL—18′ 6″ B—7′ 6″ D—2′ 8″

Secondhand reports say she was known as *Fly Away* but that her name was change to *Kidnapped*. One report said she had been lost. A more recent statement says she is being rebuilt. We hope to see her and learn something more definite about her.

31

WHITE EAGLE
Class A
Bob Montana, Meridith, New Hampshire
built by Wilbur A. Morse, 1915
LOA—28′ LWL—24′ B—9′ 6″ D—5′ 6″
3 races; 1 second

The *White Eagle* graces the waters of Lake Winnepesaukee, New Hampshire. In the fall of 1961, Bob Montana, cartoonist of "Archie," trucked her to Lash Brothers Boat Yard for extensive repairs. She was relaunched at Friendship, raced well in the 1962 Regatta, sailed to Portsmouth, and was trucked back to her Lake.

Note her big, overlapping jib.

NOMAD
Class A
James E. Ford, Middletown, Connecticut
built by Wilbur A. Morse, 1906
LOA—44' B—11' 9" D—5' 5"

32

33

She was originally named the *Result* when launched by Phil Nichols. Her name was changed to *Cyrano,* and she sailed under this name through several owners until Tom Montgomery, a merchant mariner, named her the *Smuggler*. We hope her present owner, Arthur Krause, will bring her back to Friendship.

She makes a handsome sight under full sail.

Carlton Simmons

SMUGGLER
Class B
Arthur A. Krause, Chester, Connecticut
built by Philip Nichols, 1942
LOA—28' 3" LWL—26' B—9' 2" D—5'
2 races

34

PAL-O-MINE
Class B
James B. L. Lane, Winchester, Massachusetts
built by Warren Prescott Gannet, 1947
LOA—27′ 2″ LWL—23′ 11″ B—8′ D—3′ 10″
3 races

We remember James B. L. Lane arriving for the Regatta just as it started. Word was that he raced the *Pal-O-Mine* towing his skiff, but others said he was just looking the course over.

Her Charlie Noble atop the house tells of cool nights in a snug cabin.

35

MARY C
Class B
Nathaniel Clapp, Prides Crossing, Massachusetts
built by Nathaniel Clapp, 1962
LOA—20′ LWL—16′ 3″ B—7′ D—3′ 11″

Nathaniel Clapp trucked his beautiful little *Mary C* to Goudy and Stevens where she was rigged marconi. A couple of years later Nat, Jr. brought her to see the races. We remember her with fond memories.

During recent years, the *MarGin* has progressed from an abandoned Sloop through a rebuilding, to the winner of a Regatta, and finally to the star of a CBS Children's Hour.

Note her vertical-cut sails with new cloths in the leech of the mainsail.

MARGIN
Class C
Gerald Kinney, Camden, Maine
LOA—25′ ″3 LWL—21′ B—8′ 4″ D—4′
16 races; 3 firsts, 2 seconds, 4 thirds

36

Elmer Barde

Doctor Files, a dentist, has tremendous fun with the *Chance*. His crew list for the Regatta usually reads: Files, Files, Files, Files . . . There are usually about ten aboard, all the skipper's relatives.

Since only seven show in this photo, we assume there are more below. Note the downward curve to her bowsprit.

37

CHANCE
Class A
Doctor Thomas Files, East Orange, New Jersey
built by Wilbur A. Morse, 1916
LOA—32'
15 races; 1 second, 5 thirds

Carlton Simmons

GOLD IVY
Class B
Harold C. Marden, Jr., Wilmington, Delaware
built by W. S. Carter, 1938
LOA–38′ LWL–32′ B–12′ D–6′

Formerly the *Eleazar*, she was built for three Dartmouth men and named for Eleazar Wheelock, founder of the school which became Dartmouth College.

38

39

DOWNEASTER
Class B
Doctor John Lachman, Villanova, Pennsylvania, and Doctor James McLamb, Kittery, Maine
built by Lash Brothers, 1963
LOA–30′
8 races; 1 first, 2 seconds, 1 third

She is the first of the recent Sloops built by Lash Brothers of Friendship. She tied *Eastward* in 1963 and was winner of a "sail-off" race, giving her the Governor's Cup.

Her shapely hull makes a pretty picture.

40

COMESIN
Carlton Wilder, Jacksonville, Florida
built by Ervin Jones, 1962
LOA—32′ LWL—27′ B—10′ 6″ D—5′ 4″

Originally named the *Elicia II*, she strayed from Maine waters to Florida. Carlton Wilder is an avid sailor and cruises with her to the Bahamas. She is as much at home in Jacksonville or crossing the Gulf Stream as she was in Boothbay, Maine.

She has a radio antenna at the masthead, a roller jib, a plough anchor on the bowsprit, and ratlines in the port rigging.

41

SNAFU
Alfred Gastonguay, Beverly, Massachusetts
LOA—35′

PAM
Class C
Kenneth Billings, Manchester, Massachusetts
built by Carlton Simmons and John P.
    Hennings, 1963
LOA—26′ LWL—20′ 9″ B—7′ 6″ D—3′ 8″
8 races; 3 thirds

This Sloop sailed in the 1964 through 1966 Regattas as the *Nancy* under the ownership of one of her builders, John Hennings. We look forward to *Pam's* return to Friendship under Kenneth Billings' guidance.

A more eager and enthusiastic owner and crew could not be found than aboard the *Gypsy*. Past president Bob Lash's famous laugh can be heard up and down the whole race course.

The *Gypsy's* speed indicator, mounted on the stern, must be pointing to a solid five knots in this photo.

Carlton Simmons

GYPSY
Class C
Robert Lash, Orland, Maine
built by Judson Crouse
LOA—23′
10 races; 3 seconds, 1 third

44

SAZERAC
Class A
George Morrill, Jr., Portland, Maine
built by Wilbur A. Morse, 1913
LOA—33′ LWL—26′ B—11′ D—5′
10 races; 2 seconds, 3 thirds

Clinton Merrill of Portland, Maine, raced the *Sazerac* for two years and had the honor of being the oldest skipper racing in the Friendship Sloop Regatta. President George Morrill bought her and had her rebuilt extensively by James Rockefeller. Now she is back at the starting line and doing well in the races with George at the helm.

Note her extra long boom and gaff and the handsome tumble home to her stern.

Courtesy, James S. Rockefeller, Jr.

If you have seen a Kodak advertisement lately showing a Friendship Sloop, you have seen the *Flying Jib* as she was when owned by Elbert Powell of Arlington, Massachusetts. The *Flying Jib* now boasts the only maroon hull in the fleet, because that is the color Newt Hinckley's wife wanted.

Note the cap to take a topmast and the jib stops on the bowsprit.

FLYING JIB
Class B
Newton Hinckley, Wayland, Massachusetts
built by W. S. Carter, 1936
LOA—30′ B—9′ 10′ D—5′ 6″
12 races

45

Carlton Simmons

46

DIRIGO
Class B
Ernest Sprowl, Searsmont, Maine
built by Lash Brothers, 1964
LOA—30' 2" LWL—25' B—9' 6" D—4' 9"
13 races; 5 firsts, 2 seconds

Built and launched at Friendship, the *Dirigo* was sailed at Rockland, Maine, hauled out, and trucked to Manhasset, New York, where she was re-rigged and re-christened on Maine Day at the New York Worlds Fair. After the festivities she was sailed home to Maine where she has been sailing ever since in Muscongus Bay.

The photo shows her in the latter role.

Irving Nevells

Before McKie Roth built the *Galatea* in San Francisco, he traveled to Maine to consult with Friendship Sloop builders. After completing this Sloop, plus other boats, Nick decided to move to Maine. He is the only Friendship Sloop builder who has to his record the building of a Friendship on each coast.

Here, his West Coast creation romps along. A Friendship's bowsprit makes anchor handling a relatively simple matter.

GALATEA
John Kapelowitz, Redwood City, California
built by McKie Roth, 1964

47

Diane Beeston

48

CHANNEL FEVER

Class C

Gordon Winslow, Needham, Massachusetts,
 and Southport, Maine

built by F. A. Provener, 1934

LOA—33' 6" LWL—27' 4" B—11' 3" D—6'

13 races; 6 firsts, 6 seconds, 1 third

The *Channel Fever* is the only Friendship Sloop that tows a dory for a tender. She is also one of the boats to beat in Class C.

Note her separate spreaders for lowermast and topmast. She has the spoon bow of the modified Friendship.

Robert Thing

The *Surprise* is the third Sloop built by Phil Nichols. His first and second Sloops were named *Result* and *Pressure*. The fact that Phil ever finished his third boat was a surprise to him, he said. The last two winters he has been building his fourth Sloop. Wonder what he'll name this one.

These views show the *Surprise* slipping along without making any fuss about it.

Red Boutilier

SURPRISE
Class B
Philip Nichols, Round Pound, Maine
built by Philip Nichols, 1964
LOA—33′
7 races; 1 second

50

HERITAGE
Class C
William K. Hadlock, South Freeport, Maine
built by Elmer Collemer, 1962
LOA—28′ 9″ LWL—23′ 5″ B—9′ 4″ D—4′ 11″

The *Heritage* is the other boat to beat in Class C. In 1967, the year of the fog, she was delayed and could only arrive for the Regatta on Sunday, just in time to say farewell to the departing participants. In April, 1969, Bill Hadlock underwent serious surgery, but in July he was racing in Friendship. The *Heritage* was designed by Murray Peterson.

She has a roller jib topsail and lifelines round the deck.

Carlton Simmons

51

(Not named.)
Robert Morrison, Metuchen, New Jersey
built by Wilbur A. Morse
LOA—32′

The *Rights of Man* was the recipient of the Governor's Trophy in 1968. Her name derives from Herman Melville's book, *Billy Budd*. Phil Cronin, an attorney, has always been moved by Billy Budd's departure from his ship when he was pressed into the British Navy. As he left, he shouted, "Good-bye rights of man."

She's a handsome vessel, beating out with everything setting perfectly.

Carlton Simmons

52

RIGHTS OF MAN
Class B
Philip Cronin, Cambridge, Massachusetts
built by Lash Brothers, 1965
LOA—30′
8 races; 3 firsts, 1 second, 2 thirds

53

EAGLE
Class A
Donald Huston, Nahant, Massachusetts
built by Wilbur A. Morse, 1915
LOA—31' 6" LWL—25' B—10' 6" D—4' 9"
6 races; 2 firsts

The smiles on the faces of all the Hustons at winning the Governor's Cup in 1969 could not be suppressed. This is another true family Sloop. Here she eases along in relaxed cruising style.

Irving Nevells

Bill Thon's *Echo* has the original style of cockpit rigged with sweeps. Bill never has to worry as long as there is a whisper of a breeze, but even if the wind lets him down, he can still get home to his mooring at Port Clyde.

She's a sweet little boat.

ECHO
Class B
William Thon, Port Clyde, Maine
built by Lee's Boat Shop, 1965
LOA—22′ 4″ LWL—20′ B—7′ 6″ D—3′ 6″
7 races; 1 first

54

RIGHT BOWER
Her last owner said she had lived a good life, but just couldn't make it anymore—so she was taken apart. She was a big spoon-bowed Sloop and sailed out of Stonington, Connecticut, for several years after World War II.

55

56

IOCASTE
Class A
Charles B. Currier, Jr., Sherwood Forest,
  Maryland
built 1912
LOA—33′ LWL—28′ 8″ D—4′ 6″
4 races; 1 third

This old original Sloop is another favorite. Her popularity is due to her own beauty and to the wonderful Currier family that sails her with pride and fun. The bikini aboard might have helped a little also.

(Sorry, not visible in this photo.)

Jim Rockefeller built her for Doctor Mahlon Hoagland on top of Bald Mountain in Camden, Maine. *Old Baldy* was the mold for Jarvis Newman's fiberglass Sloop, and she has found a new home port at the Cranberry Isles under the ownership of Miss Louise Millar.

She looks quite the little ship with her side lights and halyards coiled in the rigging by the deadeyes and lanyards.

Courtesy, James S. Rockefeller, Jr.

57

OLD BALDY
Class B
Louise Millar, Allison Park, Pennsylvania,
    and Cranberry Isles, Maine
built by James S. Rockefeller, Jr., 1965
LOA—24'
7 races

58

DEPARTURE
Class C
Franklin H. Perkins, Jr., Lancaster,
   Massachusetts
LOA—14′ 10″ LWL—13′ 8″ B—5′ 6″ D—2′ 4″
2 races

Departure is the smallest Friendship Sloop in the Society. Fifteen feet long, she sails along with the largest of them all. "It can't be, but it is," is the remark most often heard by the admiring public. Franklin Perkins and his two sons have sailed her from Wells Beach to Friendship for two Regattas.

What a great little boat in which to cruise the New England coast.

This Sloop is named for Doctor White's daughter. It's a toss-up whether trying to win the race or just having fun is more important to the Whites, but they seem to do well at both. With son Steve as skipper, they make an excellent showing even with ten people aboard. Son Bruce, age eleven, being a bonafide Friendship Sloop expert, was an editorial consultant on this book.

Here comes *Sarah Mead*; you can almost hear her bow wave.

59

SARAH MEAD
Class B
Doctor Henry White, Camden, Maine
built by Newbert and Wallace, 1965
LOA—30′ LWL—25′ B—10′ 9″ D—4′ 6″
7 races; 1 second, 2 thirds

R. Oliver Post

60

OLD SALT
Class A
Leon Knorr, Rowayton, Connecticut
built by Rob McLain and Son, 1902
LOA—32′

We haven't seen her in Friendship yet, as Leon Knorr has been rebuilding her. When Leon was in Friendship last, he said he expected to have her ready to go before long.

61

WINDWARD
Class B
Irving E. Bracy, Jr., Wiscasset, Maine
built by James S. Rockefeller, Jr., 1966
LOA—25′ LWL—21′ B—8′ 8″ D—4′ 5″
7 races; 2 seconds

Windward is the "honeymoon boat." Irving and Jane Bracy had her built by Jim Rockefeller as a wedding present to each other and used her for a honemoon cottage. As a graduate of Maine Maritime Academy, "Skip" spends his professional hours, as well as his leisure hours, afloat.

The photo was taken two hours after the wedding.

Courtesy, James S. Rockefeller, Jr.

Fran and Lee Greene are among the most ardent of Friendship Sloop fans. Because the *Columbia* is on Lake Erie, it is hard for them to bring her to the Regatta. They have attended "sloopless," however, and have been a big help with shore jobs.

Here, the *Columbia* slips along in fresh water.

COLUMBIA
Class C
Fran and Lee Greene, Tonawanda, New York
built by Lester Chadbourne
LOA—23′

62

63

KOCHAB
Class B
Stanley Kanney, Ridgewood, New Jersey
built by Speers, 1953
LOA—27′ 8″ LWL—23′ 6″ B—8′ 6″ D—4′ 3″
1 race

Stan and Sylvia Kanney and son David brought this Sloop to Friendship from New Jersey in 1967. They made a 30-hour run from the Cape Cod Canal to Monhegan in a pretty wild breeze, only to be fogbound in Friendship.

Her big roller jib and staysail set flying make a handy headsail rig.

Irving Nevells

Doctor Francis Colpoys, her first owner, finished off the inside of the *Amicitia* himself, and brought her back to Friendship, where she was built, to race in 1968. Emerson Stone has since purchased her.

The curves of her sails, shear line, and boot top harmonize nicely.

AMICITIA
Class B
Emerson Stone, Greenwich, Connecticut
built by Lash Brothers, 1965
LOA—32′ 6″ LWL—27′ 4″ B—10′ 5″ D—5′ 3″
2 races

64

Carlton Simmons

65

GALLANT LADY
Class A
Anthony Menkel, Jr., Birmingham, Michigan
built by Morse, 1907
LOA—33′

Tony Menkel is rebuilding the *Gallant Lady* and hopes to bring her to Friendship for a Regatta.

66

VENTURE
Class A
Robert Thing, Brunswick, Maine
built by Wilbur A. Morse, 1912
LOA—30′
4 races

Robert Thing rebuilt the *Venture* and has brought her to Friendship for the Regatta several times. On his first trip, he constructed the galley while his wife, Hilda, sailed the boat.
She is one of the few single-headsail Sloops.

Robert Thing

The Reverend Albert Neilson named his Sloop for Saint Jerome, also called Eusebius Hieronymus, a church father who lived more than 1500 years ago. She has participated in the last three Regattas.

In this view, she makes the most of a nice breeze with a member of her family crew checking to see that all is well aloft.

HIERONYMUS
Class B
Albert Neilson, Avondale, Pennsylvania
built by Ralph Stanley, 1962
LOA—33'
5 races

67

Carlton Simmons

68

LUCY ANNE
Class B
James H. Hall, Rowley, Massachusetts
built by James H. Hall, 1967
LOA—25'
5 races

The Massachusetts-built *Lucy Anne* is now a permanent resident of Maine. Owner-builder Jim Hall spends his summers in the Waldoboro area, and winters his Sloop not far from where the originals were constructed.

She looks to have a leg-o'mutton rig at first glance, but the gaff is almost lined up with the mast.

Carlton Simmons

John Rutledge keeps the *Coast O' Maine* in Kittery, right near the Navy Yard. Late one fall, two escapees from the naval prison at the Yard tried to steal this Sloop for a "get-away." They slipped her mooring before they found they couldn't start the motor. Apparently they couldn't sail her either, for they abandoned her on the shore, high and dry, but luckily un-harmed.

Here, on a happier occasion, she sails along past her namesake.

69

COAST O' MAINE
Class B
John Rutledge, Medfield, Massachusetts
built by Vernell Smith, 1966
LOA—30' LWL—25' B—9' 4" D—4'
2 races

Carlton Simmons

70

MARGARET MOTTE
Michael Grove, Milford, Connecticut
built by Morse Boat Yard, 1967.
LOA—30′

The *Margaret Motte* can be seen sailing in
Long Island Sound on almost any good day. A
couple of times she has tried to get back for the
Friendship Regatta; we hope she makes it this
year.

She certainly looks to be a worthy competitor.

When Bill Zuber and Stu Hancock bought the *Gladiator*, she was named *Downeaster*, but persistent searching established her as an original Friendship Sloop built on Bremen Long Island in 1902 and originally named the *Gladiator*. So the name was changed back.

The men who fished in her would be proud to see her thus, romping along with a reef tucked in the mainsail.

GLADIATOR
Class A
William Zuber, Brielle, New Jersey, and Stuart
   Hancock, Manisquan, New Jersey
built by Robert McLain, 1902
LOA—33′ B—11′ 3″ D—6′
1 race

TEMPTRESS
Charles Hedge, Waterford, Connecticut
built by Philip Nichols, 1934
LOA—37′ LWL—33′ B—10′ 6″ D—6′

The *Temptress* was originally named *Pressure* by Phil Nichols when he launched her. He said he was under pressure all the time he was building her. Now, as well as a new name, she has a new rig, that of a ketch.

73

DAUPHINE
Philip C. Morse, Jr., Naples, Florida
built by Pamet Harbor, 1951
LOA—26'

The *Dauphine* has wandered from her Camden, Maine, birthplace to Florida. Friendships, although developed for working on the coast of Maine, are such good all-around sailors that they do well in all waters.

74

PATIENCE
Class B
H. Blair Lamont, Jr., Lincolnville, Maine
built by Malcolm Brewer, 1965
LOA—30' LWL—23' 6" B—10' D—5'
2 races

Malcolm Brewer built the *Patience* in his place at Camden. She didn't win the 1969 Regatta, but the bright colored pants worn by the crew will long be remembered up and down the immediate coast.

Her doghouse gives full headroom. Here, she picks her way through the boats in Friendship Harbor.

Irving Nevells

OMAHA
Class A
Charles F. Hansel, Jr., Shelter Island,
    New York
built by Wilbur A. Morse, 1901
LOA—35'

PACKET
Class C
Tom and Bob Denney, Easton, Massachusetts,
    and Gardner, Massachusetts
built by Charles Morse, 1925
LOA—26'

Tom Denney, his wife, and two small children cruised the coast for a week in bad weather
on this 26-foot Sloop. Only a family as con-
genial as they are could disembark at the end
of such a cruise with smiles on their faces.

BEAGLE
Class A
Mrs. John Glenn, Centre Island, New York
built by Charles Morse, 1905
LOA—28' LWL—23' B—9' 2" D—4' 6"

78

EMMIE B
Class B
Reginald Wilcox, Boothbay Harbor, Maine
built by Reginald Wilcox, 1958
LOA—37'
2 races

The *Emmie B* was built by her owner with a flush deck, and built rugged enough so she will stand up a long time.

Note her lazy jack arrangement and the way the foot of the jib is raised up off the bowsprit.

Carlton Simmons

79

NIMBUS
Fred Swigart, New Orleans, Louisiana
LOA—32'

Fred Swigart promises to tell us the story of the *Nimbus* surviving two hurricanes. In the last one, Camille, a tidal wave left her high and dry.

SEPOY
Andrew Fetherston, Staten Island, New York
built by F. Buck and E. L. Adams, 1941
LOA—35' B—11' 4" D—6'

For her first eight years, the *Sepoy* was used for handlining, and was then converted for cruising. She was originally named *Dickie II*, and when converted, the named was changed to *Grey Dawn*. Drew Fetherston changed it to *Sepoy* when he purchased her in 1968.

80

81

Sailed by Don Priestly, the *Regardless* performed beautifully at the 1969 Regatta and in races at Marblehead. Don wanted a smaller Sloop, however, so Bill and Barbara Williams are the new owners.

She is one of the biggest of the Sloops and has an unusually tall rig.

Carlton Simmons

REGARDLESS
Class B
Bill and Barbara Williams, Swansea,
  Massachusetts
built by Fred Dion, 1963
LOA—38' 9" LWL—30' B—11' 6" D—5' 10"
2 races; 1 second

82

MORNING STAR

Ronald Ackman, Oyster Bay, New York
built by A. Morse, 1912
LOA—28′ LWL—25′ B—10′ D—5′ 6″

This original Morse Sloop has been rigged as a ketch somewhere along the line. Her new owner has recently raised the *Morning Star* from a watery berth and has her sailing again.

83

PERSEVERANCE

Class D
Harold E. Kimball, Concord, New Hampshire
built by Bruno and Stillman, 1969
LOA—30′ 8″ LWL—25′ B—10′ D—4′ 6″

The *Perseverance* was the first fiberglass member of the Society. Due to unavoidable circumstances, she did not make the 1969 Regatta, but we hope to welcome this Sloop and her owner, Harold Kimball, to Friendship for the 10th Regatta.

84

PHILIA

Bruce T. Myers, McMahan Island, Maine, and
  Alexandria, Virginia
built by Kennebec Yacht Building Co., 1969
LOA—22′ LWL—18′ B—7′ 6″ D—3′ 6″

The *Philia* was built by McKie Roth at Kennebec Yacht. Nick started building boats on the West Coast, but the *Philia* was his first East Coast Friendship.

Jerry Maxwell has already started to build another larger Friendship, as the *Tern*, a 21-footer, does not give him and his wife enough space for cruising.

Here, he gives the little *Tern* a rap full.

TERN
Class B
Jeremy D. Maxwell, Spruce Head, Maine
built by Jeremy D. Maxwell, 1969
LOA—21′
2 races

Carlton Simmons

86

ALLEGIANCE
Albert M. Harding, Kennebunkport, Maine
built by Albert M. Harding, 1969
LOA—24' LWL—18' B—8' D—4' 6"

Building the *Allegiance* was a labor of love. For a couple of years, Albert Harding attended the Regattas and stood on the wharves taking everything in. Now his own Sloop is launched, and he is looking forward to racing instead of watching.

87

EAGLE
Philip and Joanne Groetzinger, Wiscasset, Maine
built by McKie W. Roth, Jr., 1969
LOA—22' 4" LWL—18' B—7' 6" D—3' 6"

The *Eagle* is the second Sloop from Nick Roth's shop. The Groetzingers launched her in the fall of 1969 and managed some good sailing before winter set in. They plan to bring her to Friendship to see what the new *Eagle* can do against the old *Eagle*.

She's a pretty boat, waiting for her breeze.

Tom Jones

APOGEE
Class D
A. Marshall Smith, Somerset, New Jersey
built by Bruno and Stillman, 1969
LOA—30′ 6″ LWL—25′ B—10′ D—4′ 6″

88

The *Apogee* was the second fiberglass Sloop launched by Bruno and Stillman. Her owner, Doctor Smith, will race her with his son as crew. Note her rolled-up jib.

AVIOR
Julia and Bertha Chittenden, Edgartown,
   Massachusetts
built by McKie W. Roth, Jr., 1970

89

The *Avior* was launched in the spring of 1970. Her owners requested Registry Number 89, as that was their father's boat number in his sailing days.

90

SALATIA
Class D
George B. Lauriat
built by Jarvis Newman, 1969
LOA—25′

This fiberglass Sloop from Jarvis Newman's shop watched the 1969 Regatta from a flatbed trailer on the hill overlooking the harbor. At the 1970 Regatta, she will be where she belongs —in the water and racing.

She looks to be a smart sailor.

PHOENIX
Class D
Alfred E. Beck, Exeter, New Hampshire
built by Bruno and Stillman, 1969
LOA—30' 6" LWL—25' B—10' D—4' 6"

The *Phoenix* is the third Bruno and Stillman fiberglass Sloop. The Becks plan to bring her to Friendship for the 1970 Regatta.

91

VICTORY
Doctor A. Carl Maier, Waite Hill Village, Ohio
built by James S. Rockefeller, Jr., 1970

Doctor Maier, in his letter to the Society, sounded as if the name of his forthcoming Sloop was culmination of his dreams. She was to be completed about a month ago at Jim Rockefeller's Bald Mountain Boat Works.

92

ANNA R
Kenneth Rich, New London, New Hampshire

Talk about being patient, Kenneth Rich has been to Friendship to witness the Regattas for the last three or four years. During the winters he has diligently worked on his *Pemaquid* design Sloop. It's going to be close whether the *Anna R* or this book gets launched first, but the day when the *Anna R* slips into the water at Portsmouth, New Hampshire, will be a great one. Happy Sailing!

93

DIANA

94

Ebenezar Gay, of Hingham, Massachusetts, is having a Jarvis Newman fiberglass Sloop finished at the Bald Mountain Boat Works. She should be in the water by now. Mr. Gay wrote the Society that he was not an owner yet, but that the activity in his checkbook made him realize that something was happening.

WESTWIND

95

Mr. Matheson, of Wakefield, Massachusetts, owned and sailed this Sloop for years, so it was hard on his widow to think of someone else having her. But the *Westwind* is now in the careful hands of Frank and Marcelle Savoy, Beverly, Massachusetts, who plan to sail her south to Florida.

VOYAGER II
Bernard MacKenzie, Scituate, Massachusetts

This Sloop was launched from Lash Brothers yard in Friendship with just the bare hull and decking. Then Bernard MacKenzie ran her under power to Boston, where he hauled her and finished her. Bernard, afraid of being unnoticed with no superstructure, erected a Christmas Tree for a mast. A reporter wrote a story about the "tree masted" Sloop sailing from Friendship to Boston, but some copy editor, thinking he detected a spelling error, inserted an "h," so that when the story hit the streets, the *Voyager II* was a three-masted Sloop.

96

97

GAY GAMBLE

Francis Hardy, Nashua, New Hampshire

NAME	NUMBER	NAME	NUMBER	NAME	NUMBER
Allegiance	86	*Flying Jib*	45	*Perseverance*	83
Amicitia	64	*Friendship*	12	*Philia*	84
Amity	9	*Galatea*	47	*Phoenix*	91
Ancient Mariner	24	*Gallant Lady*	65	*Regardless*	81
Anna R	93	*Gay Gamble*	97	*Retriever*	16
Apogee	88	*Gladiator*	71	*Right Bower*	55
Avior	89	*Gold Ivy*	38	*Rights of Man*	52
Banshee	8	*Golden Eagle*	4	*Salatia*	90
Beagle	77	*Gypsy*	43	*Sarah Mead*	59
Blackjack	19	*Heritage*	50	*Sazerac*	44
Bounty	28	*Hieronymus*	67	*Sea Duck*	25
Chance	37	*Iocaste*	56	*Sepoy*	80
Channel Fever	48	*Joeanna*	20	*Smuggler*	33
Chrissy	18	*Jolly Buccaneer*	17	*Snafu*	41
Coast O' Maine	69	*Kidnapped*	30	*Surprise*	49
Columbia	62	*Kochab*	63	*Susan*	29
Comesin	40	*Lucy Anne*	68	*Tannis ll*	7
Content	5	*MarGin*	36	*Temptress*	72
Dauphine	73	*Margaret Motte*	70	*Tern*	85
Departure	58	*Mary Anne*	10	*Venture*	66
Depression	23	*Mary C*	35	*Victory*	92
Diana	94	*Morning Star*	82	*Vida Mia*	15
Dictator	2	*Nimbus*	79	*Vigor*	14
Dirigo	46	*Nomad*	32	*Virginia M*	26
Downeaster	39	*Old Baldy*	57	*Voyager*	1
Eagle	53	*Old Friendly*	11	*Voyager ll*	96
Eagle	87	*Old Salt*	60	*Westwind*	95
Easting	13	*Omaha*	75	*White Eagle*	31
Eastward	6	*Packet*	76	*Wilbur Morse*	21
Echo	54	*Pal-O-Mine*	34	*Windward*	61
Ellie T	22	*Pam*	42	*Yankee Trader*	27
Emmie B	78	*Patience*	74	(Not named)	51
Finette	3				

PLANS

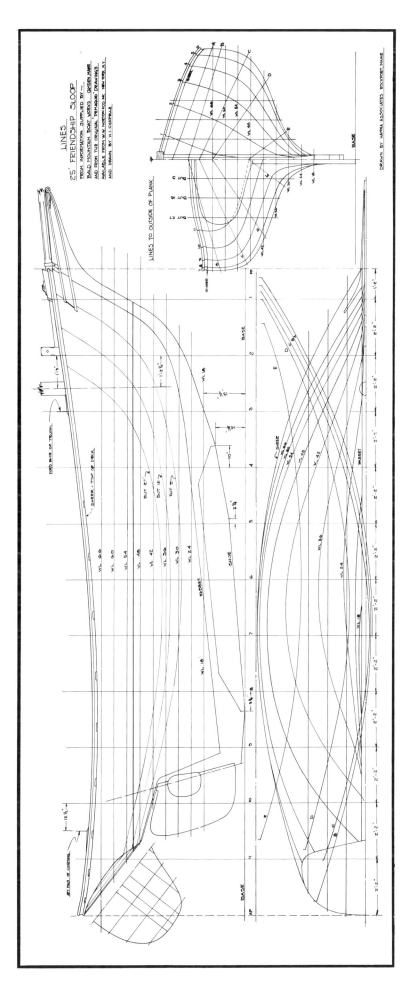

LINES
25' FRIENDSHIP SLOOP

FROM INFORMATION SUPPLIED BY —
BALD MOUNTAIN BOAT WORKS, CAMDEN, MAINE
AND FROM THE ORIGINAL "PEMAQUID" DRAWING
AVAILABLE FROM W.W. NORTON & CO. INC. NEW YORK, N.Y.
AND DRAWN BY H.I. CHAPELLE.

LINES TO OUTSIDE OF PLANK

DRAWN BY HANNA ASSOCIATES, ROCKPORT, MAINE

Jay Hanna's lines of the *Pennaquid* (Hanna Associates, Rockport, Maine)

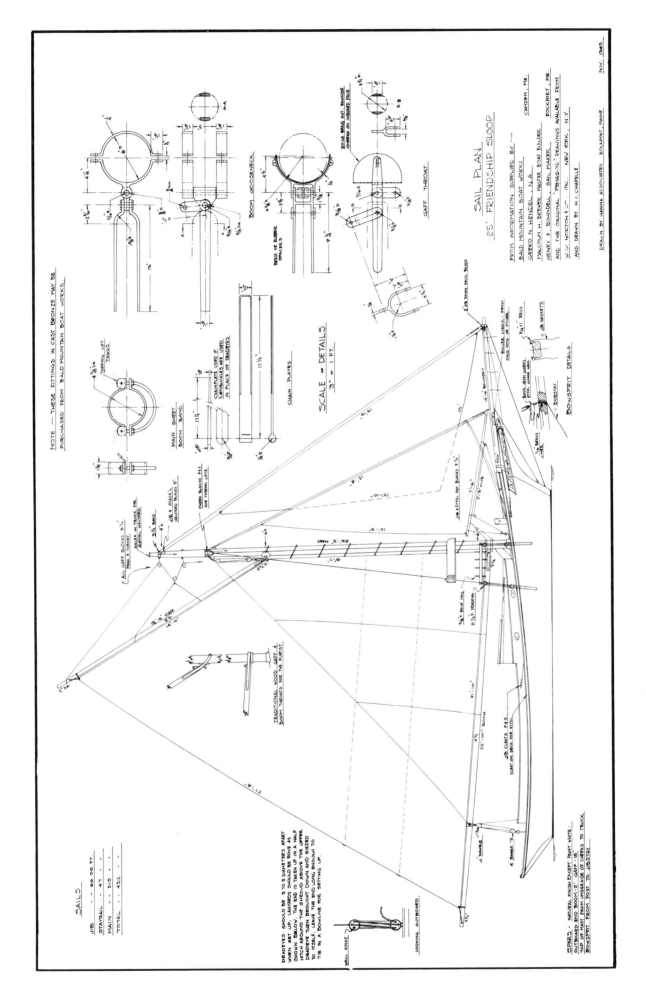

The *Pemaquid's* sail plan, by Jay Hanna

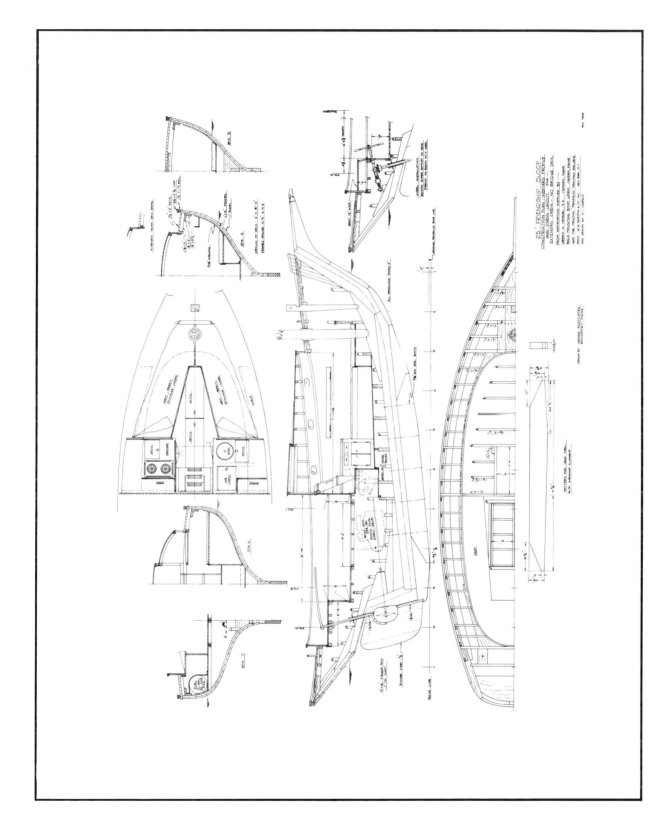

The *Pemaquid*'s construction plan, by Jay Hanna

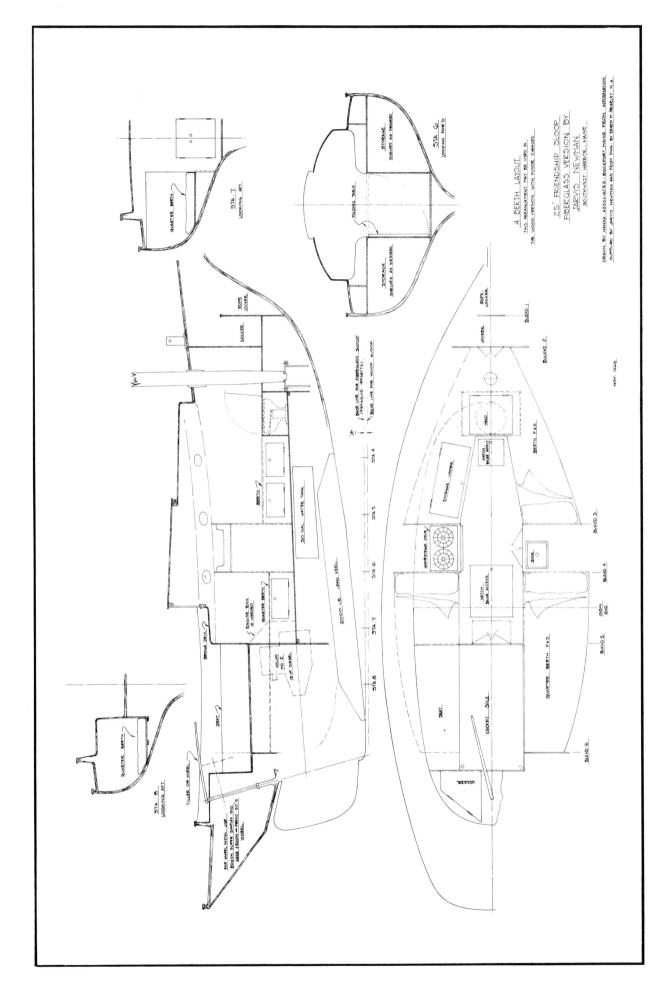

Layout of fiberglass *Pennaquid* built by Jarvis Newman, Southwest Harbor, Maine, drawn by Jay Hanna

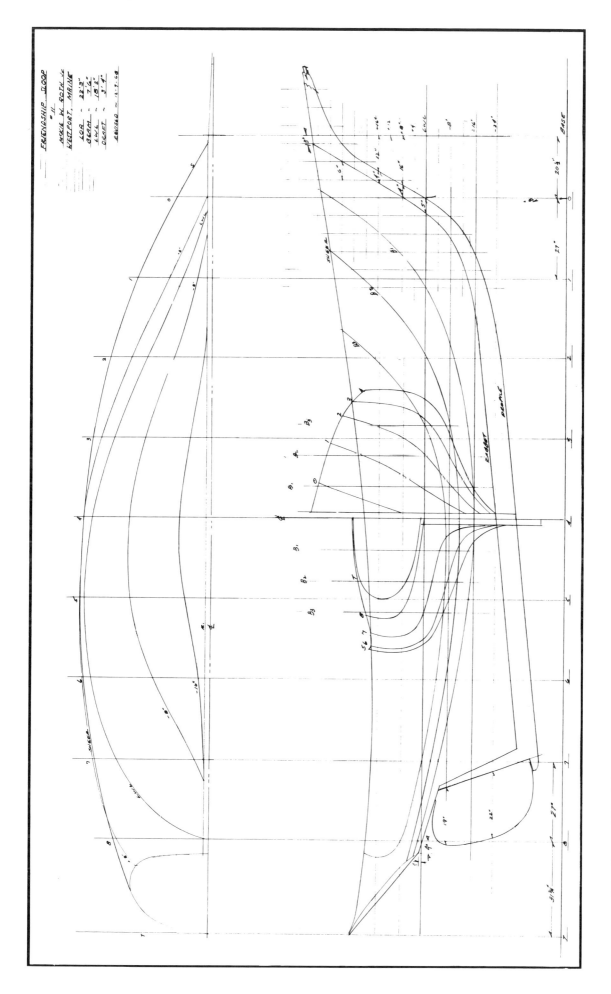

The lines of Nick Roth's 22-footer (McKie W. Roth, Jr., North Edgecomb, Maine)

Sail plan of the Roth 22-footer

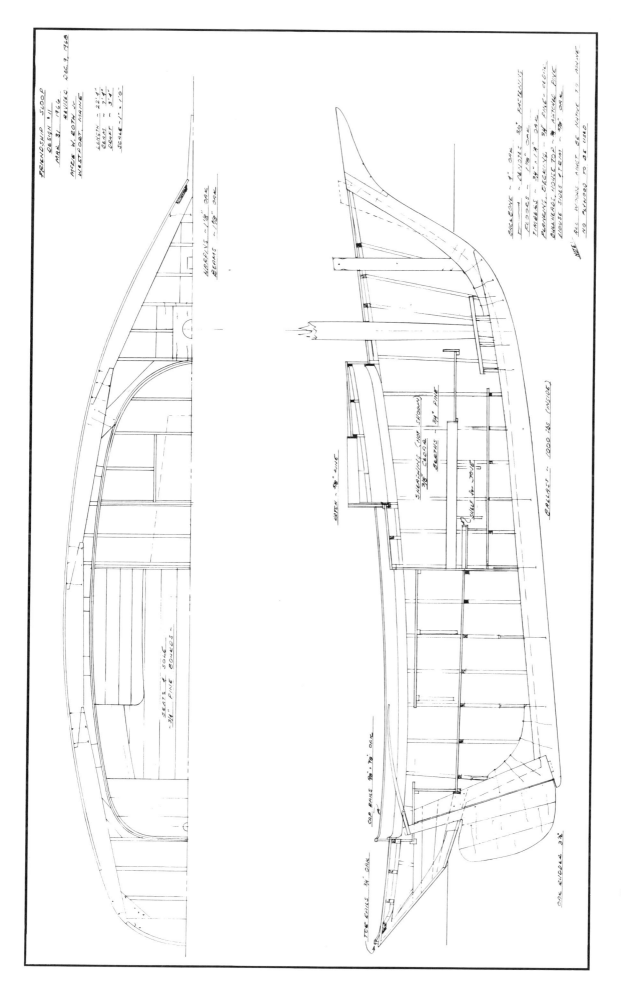

Construction plan of the Roth 22-footer

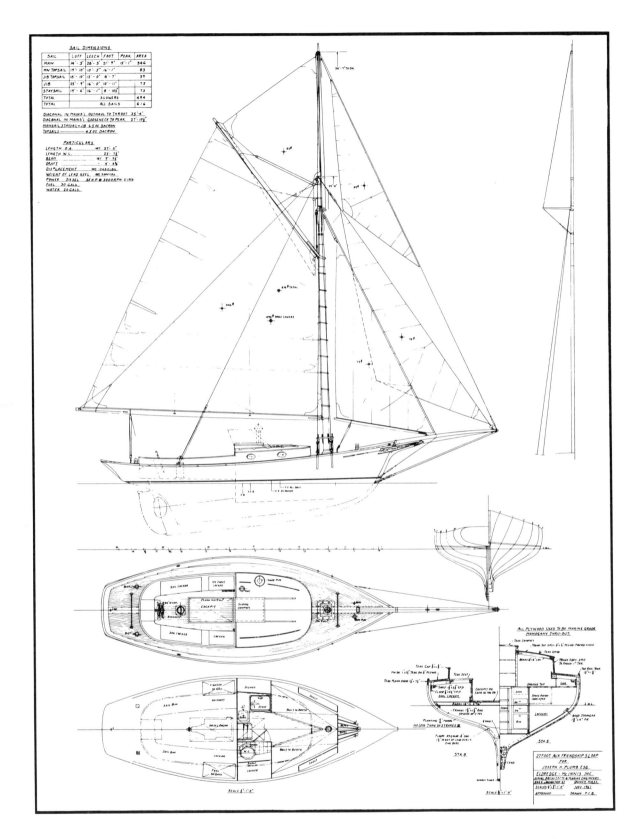

Plans of the *Dottie G.* (see page 34) (designed by Eldredge-McInnis, 57 Water Street, Hingham, Massachusetts)

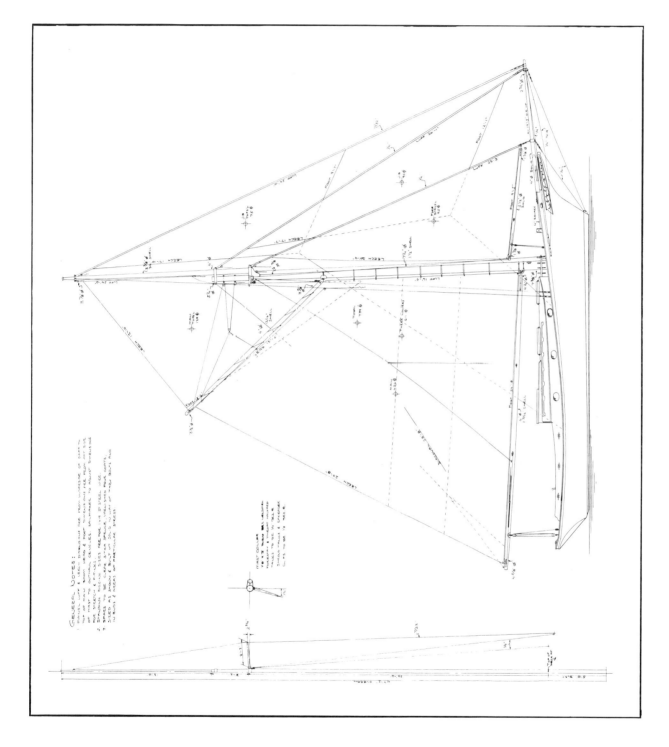

The fiberglass Friendship 30, Bruno and Stillman Yacht Company. Newington, New Hampshire

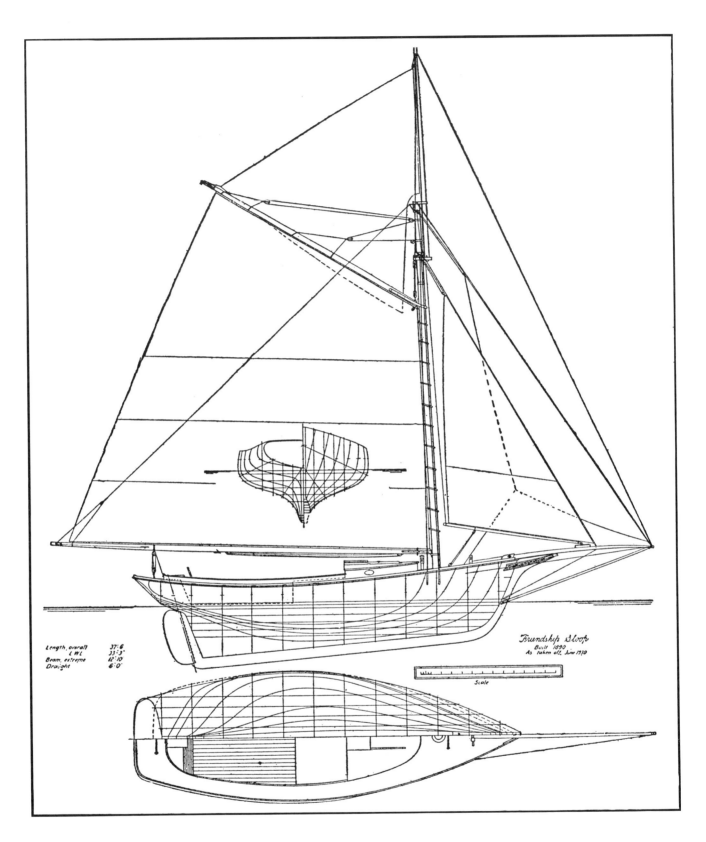

Length, overall   37.6'
L.W.L   33.3'
Beam, extreme   12.10'
Draught   6.0'

Friendship Sloop
Built 1890
As taken off, June 1930

Scale

Plans of a Friendship Sloop of 1890, from *Amercian Sailing Craft* by Howard I. Chapelle, courtesy of the author

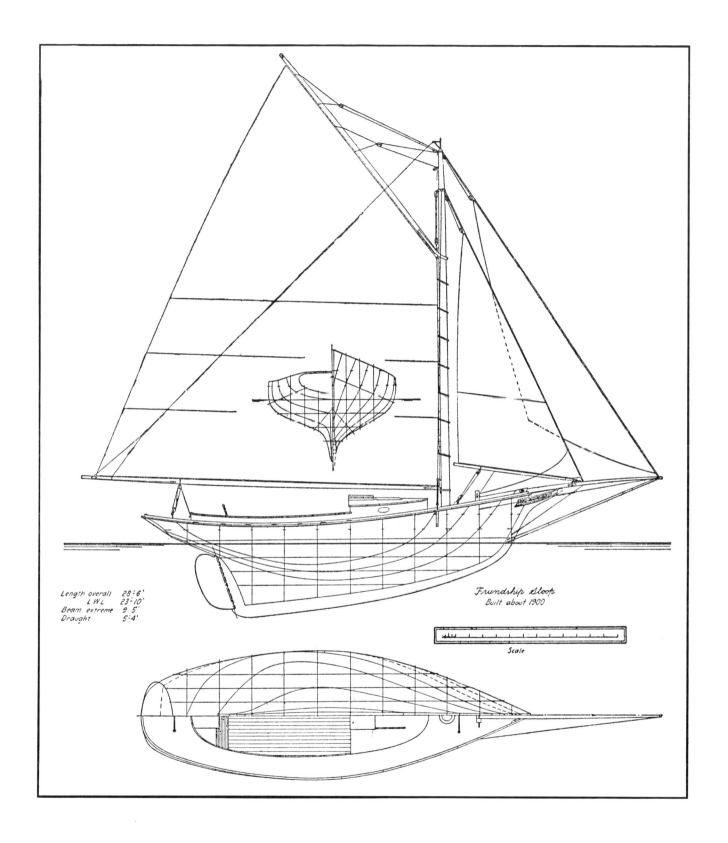

Length overall 28:6'
L W L 23:10'
Beam extreme 9:5'
Draught 5:4'

Friendship Sloop
Built about 1900

Scale

Plans of a Friendship Sloop of 1900, from *American Sailing Craft* by Howard I. Chapelle, courtesy of the author

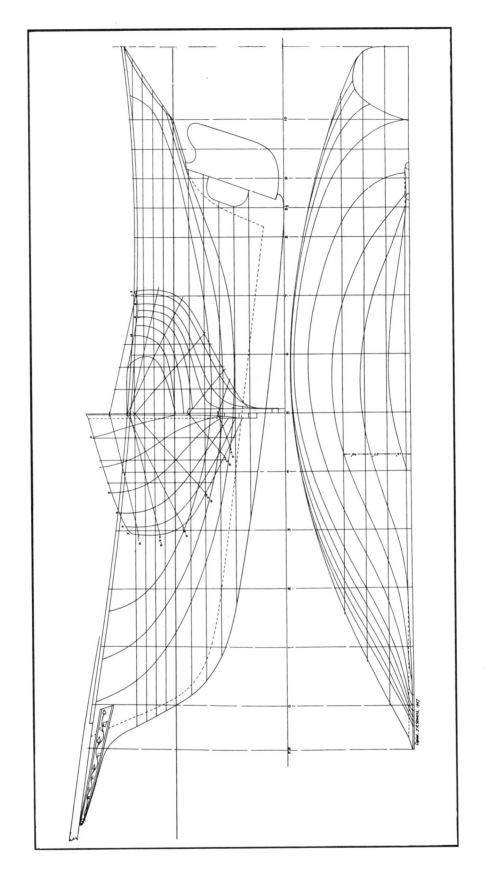

Lines of the *Estella A.* (see page 47) *Courtesy, The Marine Historical Association, Inc.*